THE ALTERNATIVE INVESTMENT ALMANAC

Expert Insights on Building Personal
Wealth
in Non-Traditional Ways

By Denis Shapiro

SIH CAPITAL GROUP

The Alternative Investment Almanac: Expert Insights on Building Personal Wealth in Non-Traditional Ways
Copyright © 2021 by Denis Shapiro
Edited by Lisa Picozzi
Published by SIH Capital Group

ISBN: 978-0-578-87223-0 (Paperback)
ISBN: 978-0-578-92085-6 (E-book)

SIHCAPITALGROUP.COM

To April, Mason, Sienna, and Lev.
You each sacrificed in your own way to make this book possible.
Without each of you, there would be no legacy for me worth pursuing.
Always remember the value of $7.

"If you want to be successful,
find someone who has achieved the results you want
and model what they do
and you'll achieve the same results."
—Tony Robbins

CONTENTS

ACKNOWLEDGMENTS

As you enter different stages of wealth accumulation, there are certain realizations that smack you in the face. For me, the first was that no investor is perfect, and even experienced investors can lose money. The second was that a repeatable process is infinitely more important than luck. Most important of all, however, is that time is the most valuable resource a person has in life. Each participant in this book gave up some of their time in order for me to make this project happen, and my gratitude for that investment can't be overstated. I hope for each person that said yes to my idea, the end result was something worthy of that sacrifice.

Thank you to expert investors Chris Naugle, M.C. Laubscher, Kevin Nichols, Brian Burke, Andrew Cushman, Bill McCafferty, David Putz, Jared Surnamer, Richard Sherman, Kris Benson, Taylor Loht, Paul Moore, Mark Cira, Dave Zook, Jeremy Roll, Matt Canning, and Jeremy Davis. To Chris Dunham, Richard Fowler, and Irvin Chen, thank you for your valuable contributions. A note of appreciation to Jenn Cirago from Emily Karen Photography, and to Lisa Picozzi, the best editor that I could have imagined, who took my rambling words and made them into a book.

Thank you to my mom Tamara, who taught me the value of hard work and frugality; to my dad Arkadiy, who taught me that it's never too late to make a difference in your family's life; and to my older brothers Serge and Oleg—thank you for raising me.

Lastly, I want to express my gratitude to Travis Watts. It was our conversation that gave me the idea for this book.

INTRODUCTION

My calendar displayed a salmon-colored appointment for October 27, 2020, at 3:00 p.m. It read: "Marriot Courtyard Check-In Winston-Salem Downtown." For three days, the alter ego I had built for the better part of a decade—the "Alternative Asset Investor"—would officially be going to work! Having joined a fellow investor on an eight-hour road trip into town, I was scheduled to visit a prospective real estate investment property and attend an intensive three-day networking event that would help me deepen my understanding of non-traditional options in investing for income, a topic that I had come to care deeply about.

I had gotten to this point because I was passionate about building my personal wealth, but traditional investment strategies had not provided the dependable results I was after. So I embarked on an extended period of intense research and personal financial growth that involved layering a series of alternative investment strategies on top of one another with a trial-and-error approach that included everything from forays into real estate and various private equity funds to ATM funds, crowdfunding channels, startups, life insurance policies, and other assets—all of which yielded varying degrees of success. Admittedly, some people had reached their destination in alternative investing much quicker than I had, but looking back, I wouldn't change my journey for the world.

For this book to have meaning, I want to allow you as the reader to experience and learn from that journey that I took on the road to becoming an alternative investor.

But first, a little backstory.

During the day, I have worked as a technical expert for the government since 2010. I was relieved to receive a job offer and get hired right out of graduate school. Even armed with an MBA in Operations Management from a college that was ranked among the Top 50 in the nation, the prospects of employment were still elusive, as New York City was still slowly recovering from the depths of the 2008 financial meltdown. Initially, the job was supposed to be a placeholder in my career. But the longer I spent there, the further my career progressed, and the harder it became to leave. What initially represented a relative pay cut in working for the government evolved into a competitive salary, and I entered a phase in my career that wasn't exactly exciting, but it was financially comfortable. As the years went by, I began to feel the pressure of bureaucracy build, and depending on my current management structure at the time, the pressure fluctuated from one extreme to another, seesawing back and forth sometimes violently.

When the environment at work became too stressful, I started to use investing as a pressure release valve. It allowed me to focus on something else besides my job, where I had little control over my hours or the level of micromanagement I was experiencing. In this new world of investing, I reveled in the complete autonomy I had over my decisions and in the potential to change my financial position by learning and implementing smart strategies. But the

2

better my investment skills became, the less "invested" I was in my 9–5.

Looking several years further back into my history, I had gotten my very first taste of investing in high school when I purchased a mutual fund that my older brother Serge had suggested to me. Around that time, he had also gifted me a copy of *Rich Dad Poor Dad* by Robert Kiyosaki. I know what you're probably thinking: how super original that I'm writing a book on investing and mention *Rich Dad Poor Dad*. You want originality? I HATED THE BOOK! I thought it was a scam. At 15, I didn't realize the power behind Kiyosaki's message. What I focused on was that he made more money selling his books and giving talks than the business concepts that he preached in the book. To me, he was a salesman that sold air. Nothing more.

Fast forward to age 33, and I'm now a big fan of Kiyosaki's work, having made a complete 180-degree U-turn. What changed? Everything!

For a year, I eagerly followed that first mutual fund I bought, checking the value at the end of every trading session. I was convinced that I was going to become rich with my $1,000 investment, and I didn't want to miss it happen in real time. As the year progressed, my mutual fund floundered around while the market climbed. At the end of the year, I was baffled when I only found myself $7 richer. Ironically, $7 was the exact wager I made four years later that resulted in my first date with my fiancée April. I met her when I was 19 and preparing to leave an ice cream parlor job. April had just gotten hired there, and I was asked to train her. During the training, I bet her $7 that we would have a life-changing date if she would agree to go to the movies with me. She agreed, and 12 years later, we are still together and have three beautiful kids. So in many ways, I can honestly say that I've built my legacy on just $7.

But I digress. What happened with that first investment?

I realized that I made a mistake. The fees were high, and its underperformance compared to the rest of the market lost me a year of compounded earnings in my early teens—something I assign tremendous value to. Thankfully, I learned my lesson and began looking at alternative options in the stock market. Unfortunately, index funds were not as popular then as they are today, or it may have just been that I was ignorant to their presence at the time (I don't discount the latter possibility). I thought the next best thing was to begin researching the best stock pickers. My search led me to Warren Buffet and Peter Lynch. They made their process seem simple enough. If they could do it, I should be able to, right? Plus, you didn't need an advanced degree to buy stocks—just the click of a mouse and a brokerage account. After digesting a few stock-picking books, saving more money, and selling my mutual fund, I was ready to try my hand at getting rich again, but this time with a $10,000 investment. I looked for value (on the advice of Buffet), and I coupled it with investing in products that I personally use (on the advice of Lynch). This formula worked, and I saw immediate improvement over my previously owned mutual fund. At the age of 18, I was certain I had solved the mystery of investing! I didn't realize why it took other investors so long to come to the realization that I had.

I rewarded myself for this newfound revelation with a trip to Mexico with my high school classmates. As our plane touched down, a position I had taken in a bank stock right before takeoff had rallied 25%. The bank stock had been down 70% the prior week due to accounting irregularities—an opportunity that screamed value to me. In my mind, I would have my all-inclusive trip completely paid for before returning back to my home in New York. One night, I found myself separated from my group at a bar at the resort. I checked my phone and confirmed the gains in the position. What a great feeling! I needed to share this strategy with anyone who would listen. Sitting next to me were two older gentleman that appeared to be lifelong friends. We talked for a few hours, and eventually the conversation lent itself to investing. Once that happened, Pandora's box had been opened, and I let them know about my "innovative" strategy and why I was so smart with that bank position. In retrospect, they were really great sports about it. They let me further inflate my ego without laughing me out of the bar. By the time my plane landed at home, the bank's "accounting irregularities" had been revealed as outright fraud, and I lost 90% of my investment. The moment we hit the tarmac, my ego came crashing back to Earth.

I went on to college, during which time I put my investing career on hold. In hindsight, not investing extra money from 2005 through 2007 was a great choice, as the market cratered shortly after. But this was hardly a function of my acumen and more of a result of a lean supply of disposable student income. The real choice was to sell or not to sell. To my credit, I did one of the smartest things I've ever done in my life: I unintentionally became a buy-and-hold investor by tuning out the news. Ironically, my school was less than a mile away from Wall Street, so while the action was taking place all around me, I was oblivious to the effect it was having on my portfolio (but I had a gut feeling that it wasn't pretty). During those few years, my login to my brokerage account dropped from daily to non-existent. I remember making two buys during those four years, and after logging in, I remember closing my eyes, getting to the trade screen, putting in my order in with my fingers crossed, and hoping that the company that I was buying wouldn't go out of business before the next time I logged in. I would then quickly sign off prior to seeing my total account value. It was a genuine race against the clock, where staying on one second too long would have had grave psychological consequences. Many investors were commenting about how cheap assets were during that period and what a great time it was to buy. Now I'm old enough to remember that "courage" shouldn't be a term that applies if you're making sound investments—but any investor that traded during that environment was truly courageous. Parts of me wished I still had some of my 18-year-old ego left; I would have successfully gambled that it was, in fact, a great time to buy.

Flash forward to the 2020 three-day alternative investing networking trip to Winston-Salem. I had been invited to carpool along with a fellow alternative investor I'd never met before who was also planning to attend the event. At that point, I had spent nearly ten years intensely researching and trying my hand at alternative ways to invest (outside of standard instruments like stocks, bonds, and cash) in order to achieve more reliable returns and increase my personal income. But in the days leading up to my departure for this trip, I was unsure that I would even be able to make it. A week prior, I sat in my kitchen talking to April about it. The days coincided with a stretch of days that she had off from her job as an emergency room nurse in NYC during the COVID-19 virus pandemic. She had been going through a grueling stretch at work, and when I asked her about the trip, I knew it would be a huge sacrifice on her part. First, she would be coming off of consecutive overnight shifts. Second, we have three kids all under the age of 5, and the "night shift"—which I lovingly coined it—is usually my responsibility. Lastly, April and I hadn't had a real vacation together since our oldest son was born. This would be my second three-day getaway in two years, and it would involve a 14-day quarantine afterward, adding additional strain on our family. It was April's willingness to say yes and the time spent away from my family that added a real sense of importance to the trip. I believed strongly in the upside of alternative investing, but if I didn't learn, network, and grow, what would I be doing this for? I would never be able to get that time back.

As we weighed the pros and cons, April looked at me skeptically and asked, "You are going to carpool eight hours with someone you never met before?" I replied without hesitation, "He's a real estate investor. We'll find something to talk about."

I went, with her blessing. And I was right. My new investor friend Anthony Khan and I talked about so many different investments along the way that the road trip became the best part of the three-day event. We have since become genuine friends and still catch up on calls when our schedules allow. It was the essence of that conversation—and many others I've had over the last few years—that I wanted to capture in this book because they've opened so many doors for me.

The people that I asked to participate in this book are some of the best alternative investors and operators in the country in their respective spaces. But they're not celebrities, and you won't find them on CNBC. Instead, if you Google their names, you'll find that they have been guests on numerous podcasts, written books and articles on their respective topics, and are considered experts in their fields. Keep in mind that there isn't a college degree for running an apartment building or a mobile home park; these people are self-taught but have been helped by others along the way, and they now believe in giving back. They weren't compensated for their contributions to this book either; rather, they agreed because they have a genuine love for what they do. In the last nine years, I've developed a deeper sense of purpose because of what this network has come to mean to me.

I hope this book can give you a glimpse into my fateful car ride without having to spend eight hours on the road yourself. But above all else, I hope this book sets you on the road to thinking differently. This is not an investment book as much as it is a conversation starter about a different way to approach investing. It's my way of sharing with you that if you're frustrated with your current options in investing for income, you are not alone. There is a different world out there that I wish to introduce you to.

Step in and enjoy.

1

A FIRST FORAY & LESSONS LEARNED

When I took my "real" job with the government, I was 23 years old. My prior jobs were all part-time positions for which the payroll tax deductions never really moved the needle significantly in terms of my weekly take-home pay. But looking at my first paycheck from the government was a life-changing experience: I couldn't believe they had deducted almost 50% of my gross salary! Couple that with the fact that I was adamant about maxing out my Thrift Savings Plan (TSP)—the 401(k) equivalent for federal employees—and what was left of my paycheck was disappointing, to say the least.

Despite seeing two consecutive years of significant pay raises, I realized that just contributing to my TSP just wasn't going to cut it in terms of building the level of future wealth that I envisioned. So I went online to research the best ways to reduce tax liability without doing anything that may get me into trouble. What I found that resonated with me was that instead of looking at the tax code as a burden, I should view it as a blueprint for how the government wants me to invest my money. They do this by allocating tax deductions and credits to areas where they want to drive investors' attention.

The asset class that stood out as offering a really promising upside was real estate, so I dug in to do some research. Interestingly enough, it had been nearly seven years since I picked up *Rich Dad Poor Dad*, but the book was being recommended so fiercely in the real estate world that I decided to give it another try. This time, Kiyosaki's words spoke to me. I think the context of seeing my own paychecks taking a big tax hit while simultaneously reading the book tied everything together for me. Where I wasn't ready for the book at age 15 because it didn't apply to my life at that time, I was now more open to the ideas that were suddenly relevant to my current circumstances—especially the importance Kiyosaki assigned to the concept of *owning assets over buying liabilities* and distinguishing between the two.

As I dipped my toe into the real estate investment world, the old adage of taking one step forward and two steps back developed special meaning to me. The "step forward" for me was realizing that passive income— specifically, income generated by real estate investments—was extremely important. The "two steps back" involved me trying to shortcut the process by purchasing an existing single-family rental property in East Orange, NJ, from a family member. Almost everything about the deal turned out to be wrong, except for the amazing life lessons I learned in the process: My cash flow was terrible, I overpaid for a poorly located single-family property, I did no market research on the long-term prospects of the neighborhood, and I experienced no appreciation while holding on to the property for seven long years. But wait, it gets better. During those years, I learned the dark side of being a real estate investor in a low-income area. I dealt with evictions, severe property damage after tenant turnover, housing authority recertifications, property tax appeals, attempted burglaries, and more. If I would have purchased the property at a better price, I would have been able to avoid some of those issues by hiring property management and setting better reserves. In hindsight, buying at the wrong price had a negative ripple effect on the entire investment period.

Being entirely new to the real estate world, I had taken a lot of simple things for granted. As one example, I've had the same phone number for the last 20 years, and I'm reasonably easy to contact. I assumed most people operated in a similar way, but my tenant was a different story. I never knew how to reach him because his phone was always out of service, or he changed numbers without letting me know. My success rate of reaching him by phone was less than 50%, and when I would drive by the house, he was rarely home. As a result, months would go by without me knowing what was happening with the property. The place looked reasonably kept up, so I continued with the status quo, even though I knew it was a terrible and unsustainable model.

The good news is that there were indeed substantial tax benefits from actively managing my own property. While the losses weren't tremendous given the low value of the property, they did help offset the salary increases that I was now receiving annually.

A few final thoughts on my first rental property. Three years into owning the house, I was forced to issue my first eviction and undertake a complete remodel. I did a lot of the contracting work myself to save money, but still ended up spending about $10,000 and two months of traveling back and forth to the house five to seven days per week. In the end, the place looked great. During the final week of the renovation, I listened to a podcast that recommended installing a security system in all vacant rentals, and I instantly got a nagging feeling in my stomach that I should not delay in following that advice. That night, I ordered a prepaid system that offered monitoring for only $15/month without a contract requirement. That meant I could conveniently stop and start the service as my tenants moved in and out. I installed the system on a Friday and locked up, looking forward to showing the property to prospective new tenants. Two days later, I received a call from the monitoring center. I originally thought it was a test, but sure enough, someone had broken in. I drove to the property with my heart beating out of my chest as I prepared for the worst.

When I got to the property, no one was there. I called the security company, and they coordinated sending a police officer over to go into the house with me. I waited a few minutes before the police SUV pulled up with an officer who was about my age and had a name I'll never forget: James Bond. We went in and looked in every room, including the basement, but there was no sign of an intruder still on the premises. In the kitchen, we found a bucket filled with water with the submerged alarm still going off inside of it. Whoever broke in had tried to smash the siren with a hammer, and when that didn't work, they tried to drown it and then left quickly before the police arrived. Upstairs, I found a discarded security guard uniform on the floor next to an unlocked window; I guess the goal was to pretend to be a guard so the neighbors wouldn't get suspicious. That alarm system cost me $300, plus one month of monitoring at $15. If you factor in the amount of damage the burglary could have cost me, the alarm system ranks up there as one of the best investments that I've ever made. Sometimes defense really is the best offense.

The silver lining to the break-in? The police officer was looking for a new place to live and loved how the renovation came out. While going room by room looking for the burglar, he got to take an impromptu house tour. We exchanged contact information, and he almost signed a lease. Sometimes, when you're a real estate investor, you start your day walking into a crime scene and end it by securing a great tenant lead.

In 2014, I purchased my first duplex. This time, the circumstances were completely different. For starters, I was working in an area I knew really well: my hometown of Staten Island, NY. While the duplex was nearly four times more expensive than my previous rental property, it became an exponentially better investment. I received great lending terms because it was my primary residence, and because I lived in one unit and rented out a second larger apartment, the mortgage was almost completely covered by my tenants. I learned that this strategy was known as "house hacking," a term popularized by BiggerPockets, an online community of real estate investors that offers forums, podcasts, and other resources that I would listen to any time I was driving in my car. It was nice to have an official term to justify my investment strategy, but in reality, it just made good business sense to me.

Because of everything I had learned up to that point, my experience represented a 180-degree change compared to the first rental: I knew what was going on at all times, I was always able to reach my tenants, repairs were handled immediately or preventatively, and the rent prices in the area gradually increased because the population and median income in Staten Island were also rising. I did not have to deal with a single eviction and still received tax benefits. I was also a smarter landlord. I offered amenities like basement storage and in-unit laundry machines to attract better tenants. I installed a security system with cameras, automated the monthly payments from my tenants, placed smart locks throughout the house, and made landlord-friendly renovations, such as installing LED lighting, low-flow faucets, toilets, and shower heads. And I started realizing other savings by using the same paint and construction materials for all of my rentals.

During this time, I continued testing various stock strategies. I traded options, bitcoins, growth stocks, value stocks, closed-end funds, master limited partnerships (MLPs), utilities, real estate investment trusts (REITs), and dividend-paying stocks. But every time I thought I was on to something promising, my ego was humbled shortly afterward. I came to the realization that the stock market was a great tool for asset appreciation, but unfortunately, the benefit of its almost universal liquidity comes with unlimited volatility which, in turn, creates income uncertainty.

I saw three scenarios begin repeating themselves.

First, if I invested in higher yielding instruments like MLPs or REITS, a quick market downturn would erase years of the yield I earned in a matter of days. To see this example in action, take a look at what happens to oil and gas MLPs. While MLPs are billed as midstream companies that are "toll collectors" that are supposed to have very little commodity price exposure to oil and gas since the companies themselves don't explore and sell the commodity, all you have to do to see that this is not the case is pull up performance records of the largest MLPs during the 2020 oil crash to see the correlation between their stock price and the price of the commodity.

Price Movement of an MLP REIT and the Price of Oil From 02/2020–04/2020

Image credit: Yahoo! Finance

The second scenario that commonly unfolded was a stock with a reputation of being a reliable dividend payer would all of sudden have an analyst come out of the woodwork and make a determination that the dividend was unsustainable. At the mere rumblings of the report, the stock cratered, and the income investors became stuck. If you sold, you lost money because the stock now was worth considerably less than when you made your initial capital purchase. If you didn't sell, you had to play the cat-and-mouse game of watching their management saying that everything was fine and the analyst community trying to prove their point. This game would keep the stock on a downward trajectory until management conceded that the reports were true all along. A great example of this scenario is what happened to GE from 2017 to 2020, when income investors lost principal, time, and their future income source on a "bulletproof" blue-chip stock.

GE Stock Performance From 2017–2020

Image credit: Yahoo! Finance

The last scenario that I personally witnessed was a great dividend-paying stock forced to expand into high-growth markets to try to create a pop in their stock. Think back to 2015, when AT&T made their ill-advised purchase of Dish Network. The telecommunication giant expanded their core competency into an unfamiliar space within the satellite business, and their stock subsequently drifted for the next five years. The "blue chip" yield was offset annually by a decline in the stock price, and the result was a yield that was more imaginative than bankable. Even today, the yield creeps closer to 8% and is commonly highlighted on multiple dividend sites, yet the stock price drifts lower year after year. This is in no way an indication that the stock will remain in this pattern for the foreseeable future, but if you chased the dividend yield for the last couple of years like I did, you would have been pretty disappointed with your total returns—or lack thereof.

AT&T Stock Performance From 2016–2020

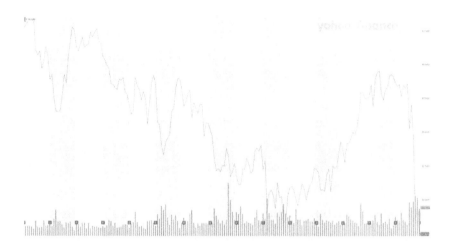

Image credit: Yahoo! Finance

These scenarios kept repeating over and over again so often that I noticed a pattern emerge:

Liquidity leads to volatility ⟶ and volatility destroys yields

Even a well-diversified portfolio of MLPs, REITs, utilities, and blue-chip payers can't escape this pattern.

Luckily, what also began to emerge during my research for better ways to pick stocks and become a better landlord was a specialty in a certain skill set: networking. But I found little to no value in networking with other stock pickers because there was such a huge plethora of individual stock research available. Even without a fancy brokerage account, you simply had to conduct a quick internet search, and you would have as many opinions as you wanted. People who invest in stocks also typically restrict themselves (or are restricted by their financial advisors) to a certain type of asset class. For most stock investors, a well-diversified portfolio means a well-diversified *stock* portfolio, whether it's exchange traded funds, mutual funds, or bonds rounding out their diversification.

So when I began to follow *BiggerPockets* and other podcasts like it, I learned about various offshoots of other alternative assets, such as private lending, mobile home park investing, apartment buildings, self-storage, and a host of other assets that weren't well known, yet all had some powerful pros and cons with similar projected returns as what you would find on the stock market. The best part was the ease with which I could reach out and network with the podcast host and guests and begin a conversation about what I had just heard. While due diligence on what was said in the podcast was still my responsibility, at least the conversation was there to be had. In contrast, I couldn't exactly reach out to a prominent stock analyst to discuss the pros and cons of his work. The ability to write one email and instantly connect with an existing investor in the space that I wanted to learn more about became like a drug to me, always leaving me eager for more.

With this wide-open playing field of networking, my investment philosophy started to take on a completely different perspective. It wasn't uncommon for a planned 15-minute phone call to turn into a two-hour conversation. By the end of the call, I would routinely have links of research sent to me, an introduction to an operator, an interesting life hack, a book recommendation, and the genuine beginning of a friendship. This just blew me away, and it occurred at a frequency that exponentially increased my learning and growth. What's more, the assets built on one another, and my newly acquired skills—like underwriting, talking to references, and doing background checks—applied to the majority of investments across this space.

The time and energy I conserved by not having to start over every time I began researching a new asset class was huge. In addition, my network started to serve as the foundation for everything I did as an investor. It was not uncommon for me to talk to an expert in one space (such as mobile home parks), then ask a question about another instrument (like self-storage), and three emails later, I would have a referral to one of the best operators in the self-storage industry.

I soon realized I had stumbled onto exactly what I had been missing in my portfolio. I knew after all of my failed attempts at creating cash flow from the stock market that I needed to retrain my mindset. I needed to stop trying to fit a square in a round hole—which is what I was doing every time I tried a new yield strategy using volatile equities. Instead, I came up with a new investment philosophy that changed how I now look at my portfolio[1].

---

[1] I am not a financial advisor. By sharing my portfolio, I am not advising you on how you should structure yours. You should consult with a professional prior to making any financial decisions.

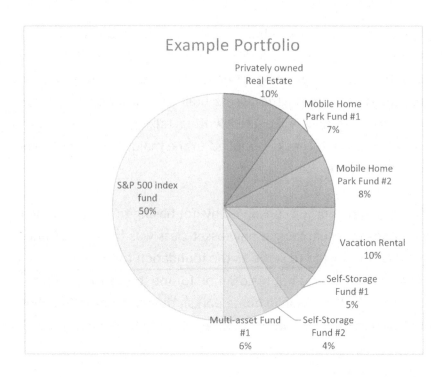

Example Portfolio

Privately owned Real Estate 10%

Mobile Home Park Fund #1 7%

Mobile Home Park Fund #2 8%

S&P 500 index fund 50%

Vacation Rental 10%

Self-Storage Fund #1 5%

Multi-asset Fund #1 6%

Self-Storage Fund #2 4%

A huge "Eureka moment" occurred to me when I stopped looking for the perfect strategy. Instead, I looked at my portfolio as it stood and asked myself: Is it too risky? Does it need to be more diversified? Does it provide enough appreciation? Is it too complicated? Does it provide enough cash flow? With those answers in hand, I created this chart that I use daily to decide what to invest in. It's important to note that I never hit the reset button just because I found an affinity toward mobile home parks or ATM funds. It was more of a self-realization that only parts of my portfolio were in their ideal location serving their highest purpose, while other parts of the pie needed to be sliced, added, or removed.

As a result, I drew a line down the middle. On the left side is my appreciation portfolio. I want to be invested in a low-cost total market index fund[2] because it is a simple, extremely time-friendly strategy, and when left alone to compound earnings, it is brutally efficient at creating wealth. However, if I put all of my money into the index fund yielding 1.55%, I would feel continuous pressure to sell. By splitting the pie this way, I can allow the index fund to do what it does best and not fault it for what it wasn't built for: yield.

The right side of the pie represents my cash flow portfolio. The deficiency of the appreciation portfolio on the left side is the main strength of the right side, where *cash flow is king.* Just as it makes no sense for me to focus 100% on equities anymore, it also doesn't make sense for me to have my whole pie dedicated to alternative assets. The two halves complement each other very nicely. Keep in mind that the right side of the pie is infinitely more time consuming to develop since I need multiple sources of cash flow, and each slice can take years to become competent in. But the time I save by having 50% of my portfolio on autopilot allows me to spend the bulk of my time on networking and researching the best alternative assets.

To illustrate the effectiveness of my chart, let's say an investor has a million-dollar portfolio. If they put all of their money into a total stock index fund, their current yield would amount to $15,500[3] in annual income. By going with my model, the annual income

---

[2] Looking at the index fund this way is simplistic because, in reality, the index fund is also broken down into separate equity holdings. For the sake of visualizing the 50% split between appreciation and cash flow, I kept it this way.

[3] $1,000,000 * 1.55% = $15,500

increases to $57,750[4]. In the first scenario, they would likely have to sell a portion of their shares every year to supplement their income if they are retired. In the second scenario, they may never have to sell again depending on their financial needs. By having so many slices on the right side of the pie, they would also limit significant risk if one deal went south. To me, it's like purchasing an assorted cheesecake platter: Sometimes it's hard to decide between the chocolate, strawberry, or plain, but at least the variety is there. And if you don't like a specific deal or asset class, there is a different "piece of cheesecake" that will fill the same role (producing cash flow) as the one you didn't like. Variety and diversification are the keys to the right side of the pie.

This new philosophy worked so well that in 2021, I launched my own alternative investment fund, SIH Capital Group, with the hopes of becoming a small slice on the right side of other investors' portfolios. It's been an extremely rewarding experience that comes with a heavy dose of responsibility that I don't take lightly. Our goal is to show investors that the right side of the portfolio doesn't have to be a mystery and that anybody can do it. I hope that after reading this book, at least some of that mystery will be gone for you, as well.

TAKEAWAY

Many investors make the mistake of switching strategies and allocating 100% of their portfolio into something new, when in reality, they just need to tweak or adjust what they are already doing.

---

[4] $500,000 * 1.55% = $7,750
$500,000 * 10% = $50,000
$50,000 + $7,750 = $57,750

2

HOW THE FIRE MOVEMENT CHANGED MY INVESTMENT TRAJECTORY

Since I started working for the government in 2010, there have been three furloughs for federal employees. If you're not familiar with the concept, a furlough is when a government employee is forced to take mandatory leave. If you are deemed an essential employee, you may still be required to go to work during this period, but the funds that would usually pay you have not yet been earmarked by an approved budget. The consequences for essential workers not showing up are severe; because all leave is cancelled, any absence subjects you to AWOL (absent without leave) disciplinary actions, which may lead to being fired. If you are not deemed essential, you are not required to work, but there is no guarantee that you will be paid for your time if you do. What makes it worse is that talks of a government shutdown have become a mainstay in today's political environment, so like clockwork every December, we receive notice that there might be a looming shutdown. People who book trips and other family events for the holidays wait on the edge of their seats to see if the budgets get passed. Usually, the deal comes through right before the deadline, making for a tense holiday work week.

For me, the anxiety wasn't always so bad. At the time of my first furlough, I didn't yet have kids, but I did have an ample amount of savings and a rental property in my name. Since discussing finances in my place of work was considered taboo, I just assumed that most people making similar salaries to mine were using similar strategies. Due to my relatively short time on the job, I was actually one of the lowest earners in the office, but the moment furlough whispers began right after Thanksgiving, it was painfully clear who was living paycheck to paycheck. You could hear the helplessness in coworkers' voices when they asked the question, "What are we going to do if they don't pass the budget?"

I'm not sure if my mindset changed during my second or third furlough, but I knew that I never wanted to be in that situation of having to ask what I was going to do to get by financially. I knew I needed to further diversify my income streams. I already had real estate and dividends from my stock portfolio, but the income they produced was not enough to move the needle. So I began looking for something that I could do after work or on weekends to further supplement my income. I stumbled on becoming a life insurance agent.

The license exam was more complicated than I imagined, and I walked away with a good understanding of the basic terms and concepts. Oddly enough, after I received my license, furlough talks actually quieted down substantially, and we even entered a period of unlimited overtime. All of a sudden, I was working 70 hours a week, and my insurance license began to collect dust. This swinging of the pendulum is something you get used to when working for the government. A few years passed, and my day job remained consistent enough where my knowledge of life insurance became an afterthought.

Then, 2015 happened.

In June of that year, I was introduced by a colleague to a financial independence (FI) blog run by Peter Adeney called *Mr. Money Mustache*—which has a silly moniker but a powerful message about living a life full of purpose. Peter is one of the leading figures of the FIRE (Financial Independence, Retire Early) community, which inspires people to rethink personal finance. While I was already instinctively practicing many of the concepts they promoted, it was nice to see a blueprint of what was working for so many others in their quest for financial independence. In short, the formula was this:

1. Reduce your living expenses.
2. Invest your savings in a low-cost index fund.
3. When your savings meet 25x your annual expenses, you are financially independent.

The accelerant to the formula is Rule #1. To see this rule in action, let's take a look at the renowned 1998 Trinity Study, which is considered the gold standard by most investors in the FIRE community. The study, conducted by three professors of finance at Trinity University in Texas, involved tracking how a well-balanced portfolio of stocks and bonds theoretically would have performed from 1925 to 1995. The researchers then ran a series of scenarios that showed how long a person's investments would last if they sold a portion of them every year. The findings showed that if a person plans to withdraw 4% of their investments each year, while adjusting that number during market downturns, their money should last them indefinitely.

Of the study findings, researchers Cooley, Hubbard, and Walz stated: "The word planning is emphasized because of the great uncertainty in the stock and bond markets. Mid-course corrections likely will be required, with the actual dollar amounts withdrawn adjusted downward or upward relative to the plan. The investor needs to keep in mind that selection of a withdrawal rate is not a matter of contract but rather a matter of planning."[5]

With the 4% Rule in mind, it's easy to see how minor adjustments in annual expenses can have profound effects on financial outcomes. Case in point: The head of a household that incurs annual expenses of $100,000 would need $2.5 million in assets to retire based on the 4% safe withdrawal rate that the Trinity Study established. But if the family reduced their total annual expenses to $50,000, they would only need $1.25 million for the wage earners to be able to stop working. This might mean the difference between a parent able to stay home with their young child or not (if they want to stay home, that is). While this might still seem like an astronomical number to most people, it might be in reach for

---

[5] Philip L. Cooley, Carl M. Hubbard, and Daniel T. Walz, "Retirement savings: Choosing a withdrawal rate that is sustainable," American Association of Individual Investors (1998), https://www.aaii.com/files/pdf/6794_retirement-savings-choosing-a-withdrawal-rate-that-is-sustainable.pdf.

others who were under the impression that their retirement number was much higher.

This reminds me of a passage in Tony Robbins' bestseller *Money: Master the Game*. In a roomful of people, Robbins asked who had the biggest financial aspirations. A young man stood up and said he wanted to be a billionaire. Across the room, you can hear the chuckles ring out. Tony approached the young man and simply asked why. The young man proceeded to describe a life of unbridled desires, such as owning a private jet and a private island. Tony then worked his magic and showed the young man how he could rent an exclusive private island with a full staff multiple times per year and bring family and friends along on a rented private jet at a much lower cost in the millions, instead of the billions that the man aspired to. I realize that this is still a lot of money to most people (including me), but discovering that your wildest dreams can be accomplished with a fraction of the money that you think you need is a life-changing realization. That's how I felt when I discovered Peter Adeney's words for the first time.

The one big caveat to financial independence is that most people suffer from tunnel vision when it comes to getting out of the "rat race." All they can imagine is leaving their W-2 position, waking up the next day without their alarm clock, and starting to map out the rest of their lives. In some cases, they leave their jobs years or even decades earlier than they expected with cliché plans that sound great on the surface. This might include traveling, homeschooling, getting back to the gym, catching up on Netflix, visiting family and friends, and picking up a new hobby or two. However, they eventually come back from the trips, their friends and family go back to work, the Netflix queue is empty, and then boredom and depression set in. These "master planners" overlooked the significance of planning for longer-term, lasting happiness. This is the same phenomenon you see with older retirees, where they pass away shortly after leaving their jobs.

After discovering the FIRE movement, I made a commitment to myself to stop working in five years. The easy part was minimizing my expenses. Besides a leased car, my expenses had become pretty bare bones, and I was making good strides on accumulating assets. I was satisfied with having a small rental portfolio, and after many failed stock-picking strategies, I landed on index funds. I stopped searching for a better option when it came to stocks. I came to realize that I neither had the aptitude nor the fortitude to stock pick effectively or—more importantly—to repeat the process in a systematic way. I decided to put my portfolio on autopilot and move on to better things in my life.

At this point, my search led me to an array of alternative investment strategies that would help me achieve my financial and retirement goals while not overlooking the need for lasting happiness and fulfillment.

3
LIFE INSURANCE & THE INFINITE BANKING CONCEPT

"There's no get-rich-quick scheme here. It's a disciplined savings vehicle where you deposit money into it, and then it takes a while to build up."
—M.C. Laubscher, President of Producers Wealth

Life insurance policies as a chapter in an investment book doesn't sound right, does it? Sure, they are a defensive strategy for protecting your family in case the unexpected happens, but an investment? Let me explain.

In December 2015, my son Mason was born. Like most parents, I would describe my child's birth as the day my life changed forever. I was so happy that Mason was born healthy and April was recovering from surgery, but then my mind immediately switched to planning. By the time we left the hospital, I was looking into life insurance policies and 529 college savings plans for my son.

It was interesting to switch hats from selling insurance to buying insurance with this new mindset. I now had dependents—and protecting them was something I took very seriously. Some people in this situation overreact and purchase the most expensive insurance they can afford. Maybe it's a smart move for some, but I was still investing heavily, so I needed to find something that was affordable but didn't handicap my family's future. Based on my prior experience as a licensed life insurance salesman and as someone who wanted to achieve financial independence at an early age, my strategy was to buy the most affordable term policy available that would cover our mortgage balance in case something happened, and then invest the rest. This way, my family could pay off our house and live without the largest expense a family has to contend with. Sure enough, I bundled the purchase of our primary home with an equivalent term policy matching the mortgage life and balance. The price was an unbeatable $32 per month. I did not see this as an investment. This, by definition, was an insurance policy and belonged on the expense side of my personal balance sheet.

Just to be thorough, I explored the option of purchasing a whole life policy instead of going with the most affordable term policy. For me, the answer was a resounding no. Keep in mind that I was only in my 20s at the time with no negative health conditions, and I knew that the cost to insure me was only going to get more expensive going forward in my life. For fear of not knowing what I didn't know, I reached out to a few financial advisors who were also licensed to sell life insurance. Even though some seemed to have the best intentions for me, some clearly did not. However, they all presented fantastic looking charts that projected out the benefits coverage for the next 30 years.

The fact that advisor commissions were involved made the situation murky, at best. One trusted advisor that I had a personal relationship with showed me a breakdown of the actual expenses and commissions of the policy. While this information was proprietary and would never be included in a regular consultation, it gave me a very valuable and honest peek behind the curtains. I'm not sure if I would call the fees exorbitant, but they were high, and knowing what they were helped me make an informed decision. In the end, I couldn't justify the total cost of a whole life policy being 10–30 times greater than a term policy, yet still providing the same death benefit in the end. The cash value was almost nonexistent for years, and even then, it was nothing to write home about or include in this chapter. As I looked over the numbers, the investment side of it just didn't work.

Let's dig a little deeper to explain my thinking.

A term insurance policy can be an expense worth paying for to offset the negative effects that your death would have on your loved ones as long as you get an appropriate amount of coverage and shop around for the best price. You also want to be in a financial position where the expense of the policy isn't adversely affecting your ability to invest in other instruments.

By contrast, traditional whole life insurance policies and hybrid versions—like universal life and variable universal life policies—try to wear too many hats; they're an expense disguised as an asset that is usually saddled with commissions that are not readily disclosed. Some of the fancier versions, like variable universal life policies, allow you to peg the performance of your policy to the performance of the stock market. Historically, you would do well if the market performs like it has since 2009; however, a stagnant or declining market may spell trouble. Either way, if you already have a large equity position, it might be unwise to purchase a life insurance policy that doesn't offer a guaranteed return and is dependent on the stock market's performance.

I came to the conclusion that using the traditional policies mentioned above would make a poor conduit for my personal investing strategies, although they may provide value to another investor if structured properly with an honest agent that minimizes fees and expenses. Case in point: Both Walt Disney and Ray Kroc[6] used the cash value of their respective traditional whole life insurance policies to invest in The Walt Disney Company and McDonald's, respectively, and I would say that strategy worked out just fine for them.

This is usually where most people stop researching when it comes to life insurance—just as I did until 2018, when I began hearing about a different type of policy that investors were using: high-equity cash value policies. What appealed to me about these policies is that they were uniquely capable of serving as an investment vehicle for investments that you planned to make anyway. The primary goal is to provide the investor access to cash. The secondary goal is the death benefit. No other investment vehicle that I have come across can be so easily plugged into an existing investment strategy as a high-equity cash value policy. In fact, I haven't met an investor yet that hasn't combined this type of policy with other investments that are mentioned in this book.

---

[6] Michael Bonny, "5 businesses saved by cash value life insurance," Paradigmlife (June 27, 2020), https://paradigmlife.net/blog/5-businesses-saved-cash-value-life-insurance/.

That's not to say that they can't be used by non-investors. In fact, in the book *Bank on Yourself*, author Pamela Yellen advocates making high-equity cash value policies more of a vehicle for living expenses, such as cars, vacations, tuition, and so on. This can be equally effective if the policy is designed correctly.

High-equity cash value policies also come in handy for small businesses and even small LLCs that are created specifically for investments. They can be used in a variety of ways:

- To create an incentive in recruiting key employees
- As a business line of credit in times of financial need or to take advantage of an immediate opportunity
- To provide insurance for partners to exit the LLC in an orderly fashion
- To provide a tax-deferred structure for existing profits
- To provide an alternative to a 401(k) plan by utilizing the loan feature in later years

My first thought was this was too good to be true, and my second thought was it would be completely unnecessary if I was to stick to the core FIRE principles. As mentioned in Chapter 2, FIRE teaches you to minimize your expenses, and these policies are expensive (I'll discuss the costs in more detail later in this chapter). However, these policies can be a linchpin to creating an alternative investing business that can be operated after retirement, which answers one of FI's biggest questions: *What are you going to do with all of your time after you stop working?*

After reading this chapter, it will still be perfectly normal to have deep reservations about high-equity cash value policies. My goal is just to start the conversation here. After all, it took me two years of research and conversations with other investors in this space to commit to my first policy because the pros and cons are stark. My tipping point was my decision to start SIH Capital Group. After that, using a high-equity cash value policy as an investment instrument became a no brainer for me for a variety of reasons that I'll explain in more detail.

What Is the Asset?

High-equity cash value life insurance policies go by many names in today's market: "Be your own bank," "velocity banking," "the perpetual wealth strategy," and "infinite banking concept" are some of the more well-known versions, with IBC being the most common term. The asset is created when an individual purchases a customized life insurance policy from a mutual life insurance company. These are privately owned companies in which the policyholders are also the owners of the company and are therefore entitled to dividends from its annual profits. These dividends have an unmatched track record of paying out, going back almost 200 years. Some well-known examples are Penn Mutual, which has paid a dividend for 170 years,[7] and MassMutual, which has paid a dividend since 1851.[8] If you're wondering how you

---

[7] Raymond Caucci, "Penn Mutual continues historic dividend track record." *Penn Mutual Perspectives* (December 15, 2020), https://blog.pennmutual.com/penn-mutual-continues-historic-dividend-track-record/.

[8] "MassMutual approves estimated 2021 policyowner dividend payout of more than $1.7 billion." MassMutual (November 2, 2020), https://www.massmutual.com/about-us/news-and-press-releases/press-releases/2020/11/MassMutual-approves-estimated-2021-policyowner-dividend-payout-of-more-than-17-billion.

can tell if a life insurance company is a mutual company or not, it's very simple: It's right in the name.

Since the asset is a life insurance policy, the insured has to qualify from a health and financial standpoint. Usually, the goal of a whole life insurance product is to provide the highest possible death benefit (i.e., insurance payout) for your loved ones; the cash value of the product comes way down the list of pros associated with whole life insurance. With IBC policies, the paradigm is inverted: The goal is to maximize the cash value in order to create your own "personal bank." What I mean by that is that once your life insurance policy is designed and funded, you will have immediate access to a significant portion of your initial investment. The death benefit is just a nice cherry on top that gets thrown into the deal.

To illustrate how an IBC policy works, let's look at the following Scenario 1 chart.

Scenario 1

		Premium Breakdown				Guaranteed Assumptions				Non-Guaranteed Assumptions			
		Base Contract	FPR Contract	EPPUA	Total	Total Cash	Increase In Total Cash	Total Death		Total Cash	Increase In Total Cash	Total Death Benefit	Total Death
Year	Age	Premium	Premium	Premium	Premium	Value	Value	Benefit	Dividend	Value	Value	w/out Div	Benefit
1	33	2,638	525	6,837	10,000	6,317	6,317	508,762	174	6,490	6,490	508,762	508,936
2	34	2,638	525	6,837	10,000	13,329	7,013	541,757	373	13,925	7,434	542,625	542,998
3	35	2,638	525	6,837	10,000	22,456	9,127	573,621	581	23,700	9,776	576,291	576,872
4	36	2,638	525	6,837	10,000	32,406	9,950	604,388	950	34,698	10,998	609,768	610,718
5	37	2,638	525	6,837	10,000	42,696	10,290	634,095	1,264	46,395	11,697	643,076	644,340
6	38	2,638	525	6,837	10,000	53,346	10,650	662,780	1,566	58,814	12,419	676,254	677,819
7	39	2,638	525	6,837	10,000	64,346	11,000	690,476	2,044	72,135	13,321	709,306	711,350
8	40	2,638	525	6,837	10,000	75,710	11,365	717,223	2,392	86,265	14,130	742,290	744,682
9	41	2,638	525	6,837	10,000	87,450	11,740	743,052	2,772	101,263	14,998	775,218	777,990
10	42	2,638	525	6,837	10,000	99,561	12,111	767,999	3,188	117,178	15,916	808,131	811,319

You see that if you invest $10,000 in Year 1, roughly 60–70% goes toward the policy's cash value. In turn, you can borrow up to 90% of that cash value (in Scenario 1, it is $6,317). I'm using $10,000 in the example because many advisors in this space say that's the minimum amount needed to make the policy meet its intended goal. Typically, the higher the premium amount is, the higher the cash value that is available on Day 1. With this policy, it might not be enough to warrant borrowing against it in Year 1, but over time, the cash value increases to the point where you have access to all of the funds you put in—and then some. In this policy, this happens somewhere between Year 7 and 9, depending on which assumptions are met. In addition, even though dividends are not guaranteed, the track record of distributions is hard to argue against.

After a certain time period in the IBC policy, that policy becomes self-sustaining. If you take a look sometime between Year 8 and 10, the dividend would cover the base premium needed to sustain the policy, and you can stop contributing. This happens sooner on a higher funded policy. However, you might not want to stop contributing in order to keep building the cash value and the death benefit, but at least you have the option to stop if you choose to.

After 20 years, your policy would have a cash value of $335,000—of which you can loan up to 90%—and a death benefit of over $1 million for your loved ones.

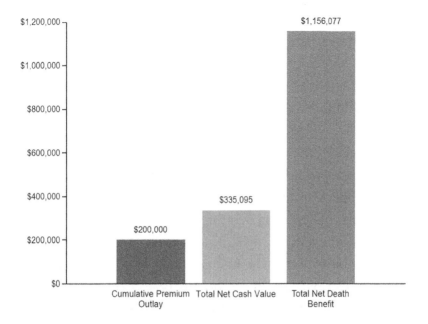

Now let's look at Scenario 2, which represents a traditional whole life policy.

Scenario 2

Year	Age	Base Contract Premium	Guaranteed Assumptions			Non-Guaranteed Assumptions			
			Total Cash Value	Increase In Total Cash Value	Total Death Benefit	Dividend	Total Cash Value	Increase In Total Cash Value	Total Death Benefit
1	31	10,000	0	0	1,063,607	0	0	0	1,063,607
2	32	10,000	0	0	1,063,607	0	0	0	1,063,607
3	33	10,000	1,617	1,617	1,063,607	1,010	2,627	2,627	1,064,617
4	34	10,000	9,828	8,211	1,063,607	2,050	12,925	10,298	1,071,860
5	35	10,000	19,975	10,147	1,063,607	2,412	25,596	12,671	1,084,365
6	36	10,000	28,462	8,488	1,063,607	2,765	37,050	11,454	1,098,506
7	37	10,000	37,237	8,775	1,063,607	3,154	49,281	12,231	1,114,157
8	38	10,000	46,331	9,094	1,063,607	3,526	62,319	13,039	1,131,345
9	39	10,000	55,733	9,402	1,063,607	3,890	76,164	13,845	1,149,875
10	40	10,000	65,550	9,817	1,063,607	4,179	90,863	14,700	1,169,539

37

Notice the difference in cash value. The death benefit during the first two years is almost double the amount in the IBC policy, but the cash value is non-existent during those early years. This is why we say the death benefit is the cherry on top of an IBC policy: Its core benefit is its cash value from Day 1.

Keep in mind that it's not uncommon to stack these policies on top of each other, which involves purchasing and creating a basket of multiple policies—but this needs to be carefully designed to avoid any singular policy being overfunded and reclassified as a modified endowment contract (MEC). In simple terms, this is a tax classification tool that the IRS uses to limit the amount of money investors can put into life insurance policies to prevent misusing them as tax shelters. IBC policies are designed to get you to the MEC limit, but not go over it. (Note: The consequences of going over the MEC limit are severe, including losing the life insurance designation and the tax benefits that come along with it.) One way to get around the MEC designation is by incorporating the stacking method. When you start, your MEC status is determined by IRS rules dictating the maximum amount of premiums you can pay in the first seven years, as determined by the seven-pay test. However, because your circumstances may change fairly quickly, you may want to buy additional insurance. An easy way to do this is by purchasing a new policy that has a separate MEC limit that is independent of the first policy. When you purchase multiple policies in this way, you can stack them to provide more insurance for yourself (or your business) without jeopardizing MEC compliance.

Here's where the "be your own bank" concept kicks in: Once the cash value of your IBC policy has built up to meet your investing needs, you can effectively use the loan option as your own personal line of credit that doesn't require credit checks, qualification, or any kind of underwriting. Loans are approved in hours, not days, and they never show up on your credit report, and your policy serves as collateral. In the event that something happens to you, the death benefits are offset by the loan balance, but the remainder is paid out to your loved ones. The loan interest rate is usually variable, but some companies offer fixed rates, as well. At the time of this writing, the loan interest rate is around 5%. This makes taking a loan out today a wash because most mutual companies pay a dividend in excess of the 6% range.

These policies do require some significant strategic planning that coincide with their two distinct phases: the accumulation phase and the distribution phase. The goal as an investor during the accumulation phase is to avoid taking out loans for personal use and instead to use the policy to invest in opportunities that need funding and can produce higher yielding returns than the interest rate offered by the mutual company. (A few investment options mentioned later in this book are used frequently in combination with an IBC policy.) The returns from these investments can be used to pay back the loan or, at the very least, the interest on the loan. It may seem confusing that you have to pay interest if it's your own policy, but it helps to remember that your policy is not loaning you the money; instead, your life insurance company is making the loan by collateralizing your death benefit. They have to charge you interest since it's a source of profits for the company in which you are part owner. This interest then flows back to you as part of your share of the profits that comes in the form of your dividend payment at the end of the year. This also means that your money is still in your account producing dividends and allowing for uninterrupted compounded interest even when the money is being arbitraged in other investments. How much of the cash value is producing dividends while your money is loaned depends on whether the company is a direct recognition or non-direct recognition company. A non-direct recognition life insurance company does not adjust the dividends paid on a policy regardless of whether a loan is in effect. A direct recognition life insurance company adjusts the dividends payable but also tends to pay a higher overall dividend because they are not subsidizing the loans. There are also third-party companies that will allow the IBC policyholder to establish a credit line by collateralizing their policy. This effectively allows you to take a loan (often at better rates) without affecting the year-end dividends received from a direct recognition company.

There are clear pros and cons to both types of mutual companies, but the main point is that you are making your money work for you in two different places at the same time: First, by earning dividends and providing a death benefit; and second, by allowing you to deploy capital on any investment you come across at a moment's notice without disrupting the compounding effect.

It's important that during the accumulation stage, you treat the cash value as you would if you borrowed those funds from a bank. And if you deplete the funds with nothing to show for it and no intention of paying the loan back, you would've been better off never purchasing the policy in the first place.

The following chart shows the flow your money should be taking during the accumulation stage: from the premiums you pay, to the investments you make, to the returns you earn, to the dividends your policy produces. Notice how the policy is contained, and once cash comes in, it flows through to your investments and then back into your "bank." This is the "control" that R. Nelson Nash—the founder of the IBC concept—alluded to when he said, "The banking function should be totally controlled at the individual level."

Total Control of Your Cash

The Bank of You

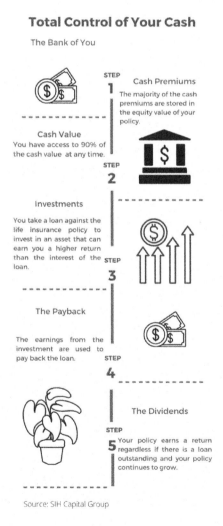

STEP 1 — Cash Premiums
The majority of the cash premiums are stored in the equity value of your policy.

Cash Value
You have access to 90% of the cash value at any time.

STEP 2 — Investments
You take a loan against the life insurance policy to invest in an asset that can earn you a higher return than the interest of the loan.

STEP 3 — The Payback
The earnings from the investment are used to pay back the loan.

STEP 4 — The Dividends

STEP 5
Your policy earns a return regardless if there is a loan outstanding and your policy continues to grow.

Source: SIH Capital Group

41

As you approach your retirement years, your policy should have experienced years of compounded tax-free growth uncorrelated to the stock market. Now, your policy shifts over toward the distribution phase. Assuming you were a good steward of your cash, you can now start taking out loans for personal use with no intention of paying them back. Because these are classified as loans and not income, the IRS does not tax these gains.

In the following example, an investor withdraws $86,670 per year in the form of loans, starting at age 71. The loan then begins drawing on the cash value until all funds have been depleted—around the 20-year anniversary of withdrawals in this example.[9]

The loans do start reducing the net death benefit, but this is expected, as the focus of this type of policy has always been the cash value and not the death benefit. Even when the investor has depleted their cash value after 20 years and taken out over $1,733,400, they still retain a small death benefit of $394,929.

---

[9] This is an example of an actual policy, but you should consult with a licensed life insurance professional for an example based on your situation.

Year	Age	Total Premium	Dividend	Premium Outlay	Cum. Premium Outlay	Income	Total Loan Balance	Total Net Cash Value	Change in Total Net Cash Value	Change in Net CV Less Prem. Outlay	Total Net Death Benefit w/out Div	Total Net Death Benefit
26	58	10,000	14,889	10,000	260,000	0	0	541,867	38,813	28,813	1,391,720	1,406,609
27	59	10,000	16,092	10,000	270,000	0	0	582,917	41,050	31,050	1,430,970	1,447,061
28	60	10,000	17,381	10,000	280,000	0	0	626,311	43,394	33,394	1,471,022	1,488,404
29	61	9,914	18,781	9,914	289,914	0	0	672,146	45,835	35,921	1,511,948	1,530,728
30	62	9,914	20,339	9,914	299,828	0	0	720,533	48,387	38,473	1,553,841	1,574,180
31	63	9,914	22,046	9,914	309,742	0	0	771,552	51,020	41,106	1,596,872	1,618,917
32	64	9,914	23,895	9,914	319,655	0	0	825,314	53,762	43,848	1,641,179	1,665,073
33	65	9,914	25,830	9,914	329,569	0	0	881,968	56,654	46,740	1,686,889	1,712,719
34	66	9,914	27,889	9,914	339,483	0	0	941,695	59,727	49,813	1,734,046	1,761,935
35	67	9,914	29,940	9,914	349,397	0	0	1,004,648	62,953	53,040	1,782,737	1,812,677
36	68	9,914	32,060	9,914	359,311	0	0	1,071,046	66,398	56,484	1,832,867	1,864,928
37	69	9,914	34,275	9,914	369,225	0	0	1,141,081	70,035	60,121	1,884,444	1,918,719
38 [1]	70	9,914	36,536	9,914	379,139	0	0	1,214,765	73,684	63,770	1,953,733	1,990,269
39 [2]	71	0	35,644	0	379,139	86,670	0	1,191,409	-23,356	-23,356	1,846,830	1,882,474
40	72	0	35,023	0	379,139	86,670	0	1,166,246	-25,163	-25,163	1,765,294	1,800,317
41	73	0	34,570	0	379,139	86,670	0	1,139,192	-27,053	-27,053	1,684,698	1,719,268
42	74	0	33,951	0	379,139	86,670	0	1,110,159	-29,033	-29,033	1,605,239	1,639,190
43	75	0	34,318	0	379,139	86,670	56,922	1,078,687	-31,472	-31,472	1,550,543	1,584,860
44	76	0	35,500	0	379,139	86,670	150,771	1,044,518	-34,169	-34,169	1,506,784	1,542,284
45	77	0	36,525	0	379,139	86,670	249,314	1,007,269	-37,249	-37,249	1,458,978	1,495,503
46	78	0	37,686	0	379,139	86,670	352,783	966,687	-40,581	-40,581	1,406,650	1,444,336
47	79	0	38,996	0	379,139	86,670	461,425	922,472	-44,215	-44,215	1,349,737	1,388,733
48	80	0	40,414	0	379,139	86,670	575,500	874,258	-48,214	-48,214	1,288,178	1,328,592
49	81	0	41,756	0	379,139	86,670	695,279	821,645	-52,613	-52,613	1,221,842	1,263,598
50	82	0	43,167	0	379,139	86,670	821,046	764,192	-57,453	-57,453	1,150,340	1,193,507
51	83	0	44,388	0	379,139	86,670	953,102	701,514	-62,677	-62,677	1,073,469	1,117,858
52	84	0	45,476	0	379,139	86,670	1,091,760	633,149	-68,366	-68,366	990,676	1,036,151
53	85	0	46,497	0	379,139	86,670	1,237,352	558,564	-74,584	-74,584	901,472	947,969
54	86	0	47,771	0	379,139	86,670	1,390,223	477,462	-81,103	-81,103	806,448	853,218
55	87	0	48,582	0	379,139	86,670	1,550,738	388,801	-88,661	-88,661	702,567	751,149
56	88	0	49,244	0	379,139	86,670	1,719,278	291,857	-96,944	-96,944	591,918	641,162
57	89	0	49,647	0	379,139	86,670	1,896,246	185,830	-106,027	-106,027	472,962	522,609
58	90	0	49,908	0	379,139	86,670	2,082,061	70,060	-115,771	-115,771	345,020	394,929

What Is the History of the Asset?

The Infinite Banking Concept is a strategy created in the 1980s by R. Nelson Nash, a renowned investor, financial advisor, life insurance agent, and author. While the concept of whole life policies predates Nelson Nash by centuries, he developed the IBC concept when he amassed a large amount of debt in real estate with high interest rates and went in search of a cheaper alternative. He realized that he had access to cheaper money through life insurance companies with rates as low as 5%, but in order to structure the deal properly, he had to purchase multiple policies. In interviews, Nelson Nash alleges that it took him 13 years to fund enough policies to consider himself bank-free, and he claims that he never used a traditional bank again afterwards.

In 2000, he wrote *Becoming Your Own Banker* and began to lecture on the merits of IBC. Countless students went on to sell policies using the strategies Nelson Nash outlined. And while his approach to marketing the product was different from traditional high-equity cash value policies, the philosophy of becoming your own bank was the same. The IBC movement has grown steadily since, but it has a long way to go until it's considered mainstream. Nelson Nash passed away in 2019, and right up until his death, he was still guest speaking on podcasts preaching the merits of IBC.

What Are the Current Regulations on Buying and Selling the Asset?
The life insurance industry is regulated at the state level, creating minor differences in policies across state lines. There are a few commonalities that are present in all jurisdictions of the United States.

> **Financial oversight** — Individual states audit life insurance companies' accounting practices and financial statements on a periodic basis. If a life insurance company is deemed a financial risk, the state's insurance department has the ability to assume control of the company. Any insurance obligation not met by an insurer licensed in the state is subsequently covered by the state.

Product oversight — State regulators review and continuously monitor individual products sold by life insurance companies. The regulators also keep an eye on policy premiums, making sure they're aligned with the benefits the policies provide.

Licensing oversight — An agent must be licensed in the state where they sell insurance and complete continuing education programs on a periodic basis. Failure to comply with state regulations would result in the agent potentially losing their license.

In addition, most states shield life insurance policies from lawsuits and bankruptcy court.

What Is the Market for the Asset?
After a life insurance product is purchased, it's considered the private property of the policy owner, and different states have different regulations stipulating how long they must own a policy before selling it—ranging from no regulation up to a five-year waiting period. The waiting period was put into place so that people wouldn't try to circumvent the insurable interest requirement that's needed in every insurance contract. After the wait, the policy can be sold either privately or more commonly through a broker. The sale of a life insurance policy is referred to as a life settlement or a viatical settlement.

That being said, the cash value of an IBC policy should alleviate the need to sell the policy since you can loan yourself money as needed. Also, the policy will become self-sustaining within a shorter period of time than a traditional policy because of the higher premiums. If you're unsure whether you can keep up with the payments until that break-even point, an IBC policy is probably not the right choice for you.

Note: Unlike many of the other assets in this book, an individual does not need to be a high net worth (accredited) investor to purchase an IBC policy.

The Bad Apples: Has Anybody Committed Fraud in This Asset Class?

While I'm sure there are some bad life insurance agents out there overpromising the benefits, IBC policies are life insurance products that are subject to oversight by state insurance departments. Even though the policies are designed by individual agents, the policy is ultimately a contract between you and the mutual company. These companies are highly rated, and your premiums are paid directly to them, which limits the opportunity for fraud.

What Are the Lessons to Be Learned?

If you are looking for an IBC policy, make sure you find a reputable agent that specializes in these policies. If the policy is not structured the right way with the right company up front, the chance of problems being fixed later is slim to none.

Finally, just because an expert really loves or hates an asset doesn't mean it's right or wrong for the investor.

The Pros and Cons of IBC Investing

PROS

- Immediate loan access with reasonable rates with no credit approval needed or credit impact
- Money can work for you in multiple places at the same time because your cash value increases even when there are loans outstanding
- There is a guaranteed savings rate as well as a non-guaranteed dividend paid by highly rated insurance companies going back over 100 years
- Death benefit is the cherry on top!
- Under IRC 7702, the interest and dividends on the policy are not taxable income
- Creditor protections vary by state; some states protect 100% of your cash value
- Deferred compensation alternative — can be easier to set up for a small business owner or self-employed individual; can also serve as a way to attract key employees
- Accredited status not needed to purchase a policy

CONS

- It takes a high reoccurring annual premium to build up the cash value in an IBC policy
- It takes years to break even; you're sacrificing higher potential immediate returns of other investments
- If you overfund your policy, you lose most of the benefits
- You must qualify from a health and financial perspective

- Because it is error-prone, you need a licensed agent that specializes in IBC
- You have to be an *honest banker* and pay back your loans in the accumulation stage
- IBC policies take time to set up; expect to pay for that time

ASK THE EXPERTS: Q&A With Chris Naugle

Disclaimer: This Q&A is provided for informational purposes only. You should seek your own advice from professional advisors, including lawyers, financial advisors, and accountants, regarding the legal, tax, and financial implications of any investment you contemplate.

Chris Naugle has dedicated his life to being America's #1 Money Mentor. His success includes managing over $30 million in assets in the financial services and advisory industry and tens of millions in real estate business, with over 200 transactions and an HGTV pilot show. Over 20 years, Chris has built and owned 16 companies that have been featured by Forbes, ABC, *and* House Hunters. *He is currently the co-founder and CEO of FlipOut Academy™, founder of The Money School™, and Money Mentor for The Money Multiplier.*

When did you start investing?

My first non-traditional investment was a clothing line out of my mom's basement when I was 16 years old. I was 18 when I started investing in more traditional assets. I remember very vividly a *financial advisor coming into my mother's house convincing us to invest $100 into a mutual fund.*

How were you introduced to IBCs?

I was a financial advisor in my early 20s, and I knew a ton about whole life and variable index universal life insurance. I was introduced to IBC in 2014, when I met two very successful real estate investors at a seminar, and they mentioned how they were using these policies to fund their deals. At that time, I was a 14-year veteran in the financial advisory world, and when they talked about it, it was the complete opposite of everything I had been taught as a high-level financial advisor. It truly made me question everything that I thought I knew about money.

What is the biggest negative you discovered?

The IRS rules and the MEC seven rules. When I first got introduced, I had high hopes of just putting a big windfall of cash in and then a very small amount per month because I didn't have a lot of cash flow at the time. But that wasn't the case. The second thing was it made me rethink how I was going to use the money after putting it into the system. The fact that I wouldn't have access to 100% of the money I put in made me pause.

But everything else about the system was perfect for what I was trying to do. The cash flow system gave me control and access to my money any time I wanted it. I could use my money in real estate deals, to buy cars, or to pay down debts. I could use all the available money I had in there, and still earn interest and dividends on the money in my account. I had never known any other vehicle like IBC policies, and I came from this business. No other vehicle in the world that I was aware of would allow me to have access to use my money while still paying the interest in dividends on the money that I took out. That was the most miraculous thing. The second thing was, being in real estate, liability protection was always on the forefront of my mind. So when I found out that these policies were protected against judgments and liens, I was hooked. On top of that, the tax advantages that came along with it were very attractive to me and what I was doing.

When I got into it, I absolutely knew what I was going to use the money for. Because the biggest thing about IBC is it's not a vehicle designed to just put your money into it and leave it sitting there like we're taught to do with everything else—401(k)s, stocks, and mutual funds. When I heard about these policies, I was highly in debt. I modeled a plan where If I put money into this specially designed and engineered whole life banking policy, I immediately would have access to roughly 60% of my money. I could take that money to start paying off my credit cards. I started with my lowest balance card, and when that was paid off, I moved on to my next lowest balance credit card, commonly known as the "Dave Ramsey Snowball method."

I started with a Visa that I had. And I remember this vividly, I paid 24.99% annual interest on that card. I was making $200 monthly payments that were just above the minimum amount due. I put the money into this specially designed whole life policy, then I took the money out in the first 30 days and paid down the Visa card. At first, I didn't have enough to pay off the entire balance, but I paid down as much I could. That dropped my minimum payment from $200 to $80 a month, saving me $120 a month. I took the difference and put it back into my policy as a loan repayment. The insurance company was charging me 5% interest for the loan, but I made all or most of that back in interest and dividends that the insurance company was paying me. I paid myself back the same amount I was paying to Visa, effectively making 24.99% on that $120 every single month in the process and keeping control of that money in my personal bank, as opposed to Visa's balance sheet. That's when I came to the realization that I was the bank. And all I was doing is taking back the money that I used to give to the banking institutions. I did this over and over again, increasing the velocity over time. All the money that I was giving away was now coming back into my bank. It completely changed my perception of how money worked.

What is your most memorable experience in this asset class?

My favorite particular case study is Joseph, a high net-worth gentleman that I met through real estate investing. He's the classic naysayer. I showed him this concept, and he was really excited but he's very analytical, so he started dissecting all the negatives and talked himself out of it. We kept in touch and every few months, we would talk about the policies. This went on for a year and a half. What I didn't know was that Joseph was still trying to make sense of the process. In his mind, I was missing something when I was explaining it to him. Well, Joseph went out and bought new cars for himself and his wife. The moment he wrote the $120,000 check for those two vehicles and handed it to the dealership, he realized that he just lost control of $120,000 to get these two assets that were going to depreciate. He thought about how I had told him that if he had put the money into an IBC policy first, he would have earned interest on that money for the rest of his life. Fast forward to now:

Joseph has three IBC policies and is working on his fourth one. There's not a thing that he does in his life that he doesn't run through these polices. That is one of the coolest success stories because he was the guy that poked holes in the strategy every which way, and now there's not a thing he does that he doesn't use it for. That's one of hundreds of examples, but I think that's a fun one.

What is a common misconception about IBCs?

There are a few big ones out there. A lot of people hear from the TV financial gurus that whole life insurance is the worst investment they can put their money into. They are 100% correct, but the misconception is that the policy is actually an investment. The policy puts financial control back in your hands so you can make other investments, not just buy and hold the actual policy.

The other misconception is people start thinking that this is the silver bullet and is the answer to everything. There is no silver bullet. I like what Ted Bennett calls it—the "Swiss Army Knife of the financial world"—because it does a lot of things well.

The last misconception is people think that this is about a product that is a specially designed and engineered whole life policy. That's not even close to the truth. What we're talking about is nothing more than a process that allows us to mimic what the banks do. The easiest way to put this is it's a process of taking back the banking functions into your own life. That's it. You're literally taking what the bank does every single day into your private life and doing the exact same thing with your money.

What is the most important thing an investor should know when considering an IBC?

Use a company that specifically deals with this type of policy; otherwise, you're never going to get off the ground. The other thing is to be careful who you listen to about IBC and life insurance, as a whole. You have to find a large mutually owned insurance company that has a long history of consecutively paying dividends that offers a whole life insurance policy that will work for this, which not many do.

What is your professional background, and how did it affect your investing career?

I was a financial advisor and started my career at a very large mutually owned insurance company. I learned a lot about whole life policies, as well as how mutually owned insurance operate internally, and how conservative and how large they really are. I had a very strong comfort level with them over Wall Street firms or banks. While they taught me how to sell whole life insurance as a life insurance vehicle, they never showed me that the banks and the corporations of the world use these policies in a completely different way (bank-owned life insurance or company-owned life insurance). I think that hurt me. I was very slow to come around to understanding that it could actually work this way and subsequently missed out on 16 years of using this tool.

What information sources have been the most influential for you?

Think and Grow Rich *by Napoleon Hill*
Becoming Your Own Banker *by R. Nelson Nash*

Who that you personally know do you most respect in business, and why?

One of my mentors, Greg Herlean. The reason I respect him is he's one of the first investors (who was very successful) that I saw using an IBC policy. He was the first to teach me the quote that "the ultimate in real estate is being the bank". At the time, he was referring to self-directed IRAs, but he was the first one I ever heard explain it that way.

You are at a holiday party and asked what you do for a living. What do you say?

I solve people's money problems.

What is the best piece of investing advice that you've ever received?

Don't get into the weeds (a.k.a. analysis by paralysis).

What's your greatest alternative investment failure, and what would you do differently?

if I could go back, the biggest thing I would have done differently is focus on my education. I dove in thinking I knew what I didn't know. I would have understood that banks aren't necessarily your friends and can become adversaries when times get tough. There are different ways to buy real estate, and my greatest alternative investment failure was my early real estate investments from 2009 to 2014. I was buying apartment buildings for pennies on the dollar, and I lost them all five years later because I didn't have the right *method of purchasing the investments in the first place. You have to learn the hard way, and that's what I did.*

In five years, do you still see yourself investing in this niche?

Yes, I expect at a much higher level. From what I've seen, when you get the cost of insurance rolled in and the health factors, 65 is the golden age where it becomes much more difficult to create an IBC policy. At that point, we start talking to clients not about being the insured on the policy, but about them just being the owner of the policy and insuring someone they have equitable interest in, like a family member or business partner.

ASK THE EXPERTS: Q&A With M.C. Laubscher

Disclaimer: This Q&A is provided for informational purposes only. You should seek your own advice from professional advisors, including lawyers, financial advisors, and accountants, regarding the legal, tax, and financial implications of any investment you contemplate.

M.C. Laubscher is a wealth strategist, educator, and cash flow coach. He is also the creator and host of the popular and top-rated business and investing podcast Cashflow Ninja *and President of Producers Wealth, a wealth-creation firm helping clients in 50 states implement holistic wealth creation strategies.*

When did you start investing?

In 2001. I just read Rich Dad Poor Dad, *and it changed my paradigm on money and investing. Shortly after, I purchased my first real estate property. Looking back now, I realize how lucky I was. After paying all expenses associated with the property and collecting the rent, cash flowed. That additional money was a huge life-changing moment for me because I looked at the process and said, "How many times can I do this over and over again?"*

How were you introduced to IBCs?

I made it an annual goal to read Rich Dad Poor Dad. *Every time I read it, I found something new in it. One of the things that I picked up during the fourth or the fifth time is this is actually a book about accounting. There's a lot of financial statements illustrated in the book. And then I started thinking about financial statements and looking at assets and liabilities. The one thing that started to really become clear to me is that there's a debtor statement, and then there's a creditor statement. I realized that all of the different liabilities that I had were someone else's assets. And I started looking at whose assets were the liabilities that I had, and it was the bank. I started to realize, I was looking at all of the pieces on the chessboard, but I didn't really see who is the person that owns the chessboard. And those were the banks. So I read up as much as I could to learn more about monetary and fiscal policy, the global financial system, and the global banking system.*

It started to become crystal clear that banks were the power players in this game of money because they invented the game. I figured I had to become my own banker. I asked myself, "How can I use the same banking principles and utilize that in my own life?"

Some of the things that I learned from the way banks operate were that they have a constant stream of capital coming into them. People deposit money into a bank, and the bank then uses the low cost of capital—because banks essentially don't really pay a lot of returns these days on the deposits they receive—to create assets like mortgages, student loans, business loans, credit cards, car loans, that pay them a significant return on the back end. Banks control the flow of capital in and out, and they profit from it.

This was a pretty powerful a-ha moment for me. I started looking at how I can emulate that control of cash flow. Then I came across Becoming Your Own Banker by R. Nelson Nash. It was a game-changing book that really showed me how I could actually use a dividend-paying whole life insurance policy structured specifically for max cash value with a mutual insurance company, and utilize that vehicle to implement the same powerful principles that banks use.

What is the biggest negative you discovered?

It's still a life insurance policy. There's no get-rich-quick scheme here. It's a disciplined savings vehicle where you deposit money into it, and then it takes a while to build up. That means in the short run, you will have less cash. However, eventually, the policy breaks even and in the long run, the policy's cash value will far exceed your contributions.

What is your most memorable experience in this asset class?

When we had the COVID-19 pandemic in 2020, and the stock market crashed almost 40%, investors became overwhelmed with uncertainty, not knowing what happens next. Countries and businesses were being locked down, and unemployment skyrocketed overnight. If you had all of your money in real estate, you found yourself in a very illiquid market very quickly, with no idea if renters would pay their rent. There were also questions about the ability to access credit lines, and most folks didn't know the answer.

But I knew that I could access the money in my IBC policy, and I did so as often as I needed to. I was able to get it very quickly. While the world was full of uncertainty and fear, I was able to get access to my capital. That's what it has provided for me: certainty, predictability, security, and the peace of mind that comes along with it. I knew the cash was going to be there. It's life insurance. It's been around for a long time. It's going to stick around for a long time after we're gone. It just does what it's supposed to do.

What is a common misconception about IBCs?

It is the life insurance stigma. In movies, nobody likes life insurance because the company only pays when somebody dies. Well, there's a massive difference between death insurance and life insurance. Death insurance pays out only when somebody dies. But what they don't know, because there's not a lot of information about this vehicle, is that the IBC policy is one of the greatest vehicles that can be used while you're still alive for savings, for saving for retirement, for warehousing capital, for setting up private pensions for yourself or savings accounts for your children. All of these benefits are under *one roof. Not a lot of folks know the power of this vehicle and how to use it as part of a strategy.*

What is the most important thing an investor should know when considering an IBC?

The policy should be set up with the right company with the right agent. If structured correctly, the policy owner should be able to access as much as 70% of their premiums within 30 days of creating the policy.

What is your professional background, and how did it affect your investing career?

I have a bachelor's degree in history and economics and an MBA in finance. Besides my educational background, I think my sports background played a huge role in my success. I basically modeled everything that I do in business and investing on the key pillars that made me successful as an athlete: I studied what the best players in my position were doing—their nutrition, strength and conditioning, how they recover, how they spend their time, and what they do on their off days. I looked at them on the field, how they played, and I broke down hours of tape to see how I could improve my own ability to play the sport. I ended up playing semi-professional rugby and was a fill-in on the United States men's national team.

I am also a huge believer in surrounding yourself with great coaches. My coaches have been instrumental to my growth.

What information sources have been the most influential for you?

Rich Dad Poor Dad *by Robert Kiyosaki*
The Creature From Jekyll Island *by G. Edward Griffin*
Becoming Your Own Banker *by R. Nelson Nash*
The 10x Rule *by Grant Cardone*

Also, I learn from every single interview in my podcast, Cash Flow Ninja. *It's an unfair advantage because you get access to the top people in their space that are absolutely crushing it.*

Who that you personally know do you most respect in business, and why?

I really respect Dan Sullivan. He is a great business strategist and my personal strategic coach. He provides me a great framework for evaluating and solving issues. I study everything I can from him. He's been an enormous influence on a lot of stuff that I do. I also really respect Toby Hecht, a business philosopher from the Aji Network. He has helped me craft a strategic and tactical implementation of various business strategies that I was able to directly apply to my business and see measurable results.

You are at a holiday party and asked what you do for a living. What do you say?

Entrepreneur and investor.

What is the best piece of investing advice that you've ever received?

You can have the best policy, the best agents, and the best team around you—but if you're not an honest banker, all that is wasted. The big success in the infinite banking strategy comes down to the individual and how they utilize the policy.

What's your greatest alternative investment failure, and what would you do differently?

A mentor once said to me, MC, there's only two reasons a person fails. It's either a mindset or a strategy issue. Hearing that was a game changer. After failures, I now reflect: Was it a mindset issue? Or was it a strategy issue? You'd be surprised. It's one or the other most of the time for me.

When my business was stuck in the doldrums three years ago, I was beating myself up and couldn't understand why I was stuck and not going to the next level. It was because my mindset was still playing small. When I changed my mindset, my business finally grew to the next level.

In five years, do you still see yourself investing in this niche?

I've been doing this over a decade, and I will continue to do this. I love sharing what I learn with others and helping others implement this very powerful strategy themselves. I enjoy challenging existing societal beliefs and misinformation around concepts such as money, saving, investing, wealth, and retirement.

TAKEAWAYS

- This strategy is not right for everyone. You need a strong financial foothold with a long-term strategic plan to make it work.
- This is less of an investment, and more of a tax-friendly investment vehicle.
- You need access to investments that can produce returns in excess of the loan interest rate to take advantage of collateralization.
- Overfunding is detrimental because of the negative tax consequences.
- There is a long list of pros and cons.
- Only you know if this approach–and the timing–are a good fit for you.

4
LIFE INSURANCE SETTLEMENTS

"This might be the best investment you've never heard of."
—Kevin Nichols, private equity fund manager

At this point, you're probably thinking, *Really, more life insurance investments? Are you sure you're not a life insurance salesman?* I promise you not only that my life insurance license has expired, but also that this is a completely different type of asset than Chapter 3's IBC policies. In fact, the only similarity is that the underlying asset is a life insurance policy.

Where a high-equity cash value policy is more of a high-yielding cash flow management account, a life insurance settlement has a more traditional risk vs. reward profile, where you are investing a certain amount of money in an individual life insurance policy or a fund that purchases multiple policies in exchange for potential returns after a stated period. Investors can begin with one investment and later add to their portfolios with more funds, fractional policies, or individual policies when they have reached a certain level of competence in the asset class.

In the case of investing in a fund, you'll find that they often purchase a consistent type of policy held by individuals with a similar age profile (for example, a minimum age of 91). This way, the fund can establish a model for returns based on the average life expectancy remaining of the underwritten group.

PRO TIP: *If you see a fund that invests in various population segments instead of focusing on one specific group, that's probably a red flag that the fund isn't being selective enough.*

When your fund experiences a capital event, the disbursements that follow are guaranteed by highly rated insurance companies, including some of the same esteemed companies mentioned in Chapter 3. These ratings are established by multiple agencies, including AM Best, S&P, Moody's, and Fitch Ratings.

While the agencies all use slightly different metrics to develop those ratings, the most common are:

- How safe is the company's balance sheet?
- What is the risk/reward profile of the investments made by the company?
- How solvent is the company?
- How much leverage is the company taking on?
- What actions are in place to mitigate risks?

In order to be able to compare the ratings among different rating agencies, a composite score was created called the Comdex ranking, which is based on the combined rankings. Where individual agencies have a letter system with different variations for quality (such as A+ vs. A++, or A1 vs. Aa3), the Comdex ranking has a simple numerical assignment of value from 1–100. As of January 2020, a few companies, like Northwestern Mutual and New York Life, had perfect scores, and at least 25 other companies had a rating of at least 90 or above. For context, as of this writing, Disney currently has a BBB+ S&P rating, which is lower than all 25 life insurance companies. To be fair, Disney did suffer a COVID-related debt downgrade, but even with its previous A rating, this would be lower than the 25 insurance companies.

What attracted me initially to this asset class is its low correlation to the stock market. While I'm hesitant to say that this asset class has *zero* correlation—because if the stock market collapsed to unimaginable levels, there would be negative effects on the financial longevity of any insurance company—it still has a significantly lower correlation to the market than other more well-known assets. Ultimately, whether or not the market is in a bear or bull mode, it's a fact of life that people eventually die. And I think that's a much safer investment philosophy than trying to guess the short-term direction of the market.

What Is the Asset?
Here is the SEC description:

In a "life settlement" transaction, a life insurance policy owner sells his or her policy to an investor in exchange for a lump sum payment. The amount of the payment from the investor to the policy owner is generally less than the death benefit on the policy, but more than its cash surrender value. The dollar amount offered by the investor usually takes into account the insured's life expectancy (age and health) and the terms and conditions of the insurance policy.[10]

At the end of a traditional transaction, the investor is responsible for any premium payments going forward in exchange for the rights to receive the policyholder's full death benefit. Alternatively, there is a hybrid transaction called a retained death benefit, where the policyholder negotiates to keep a portion of their death benefit. Usually, the initial settlement is lower in a retained death benefit transaction.

The typical investor in life insurance settlements is a high net worth individual, a hedge fund, or a private equity fund that is drawn to the asset because it has a built-in appreciation component since as people age, they statistically get closer to death. This provides a natural hedge to other investments. (Note: I would be remiss if I didn't acknowledge that when people hear words like "private equity" and "hedge funds" mentioned in this asset space, they often conjure mental images of Gordon Gekko giving his infamous "greed is good" speech in the 1987 movie *Wall Street*.)

Despite the sometimes-negative perception of this asset class, many deeply revered investment professionals invest in life insurance policies—including Warren Buffet and his highly

---

[10] "Investor bulletin on life settlements," U.S. Securities and Exchange Commission (January 1, 2011), https://www.sec.gov/investor/alerts/lifesettlements-bulletin.htm.

respected multinational conglomerate Berkshire Hathaway. In his 2004 Annual Report, Buffet wrote:

"Berkshire purchases life insurance policies from individuals and corporations who would otherwise surrender them for cash. As the new holder of the policies, we pay any premiums that become due and ultimately—when the original holder dies—collect the face value of the policies.

The original policyholder is usually in good health when we purchase the policy. Still, the price we pay for it is always well above its cash surrender value ("CSV"). Sometimes the original policyholder has borrowed against the CSV to make premium payments. In that case, the remaining CSV will be tiny and our purchase price will be a large multiple of what the original policyholder would have received, had he cashed out by surrendering it."[11]

It's clear from Buffet's words that life insurance settlements don't represent a "boiler room" or high-pressure sales scenario. Both the seller and the investor *can* win in these transactions. Usually, surrendering a policy or letting it lapse is a worse alternative for the policyholder—and, in some cases, the seller receives up to four times their policy's cash surrender value.[12]

---

[11] Warren E. Buffett, *Berkshire Hathaway annual report* (February 28, 2005), https://www.berkshirehathaway.com/letters/2004ltr.pdf.

[12] "Life settlement investments: Pros and cons and facts," Partners 4 Prosperity LLC (May 19, 2017), http://partners4prosperity.com/life-settlement-investments-pros-and-cons-facts-faqs/

A subset of the life settlement industry is viatical settlements. Where traditional life insurance settlement transactions focus on specific age groups, viatical settlements focus on the chronic or terminally ill. These policies are generally sold at a very high premium because the returns should be realized sooner. While there are definitely some ethical and moral questions to consider here, the reality is that the transaction is mutually beneficial to both parties. These settlements allow the policyholder to handle their estate while living, possibly pay for medical treatments, and generally improve their quality of life in the remaining time that they have. And keep in mind that policyholders usually don't sell unless they have a genuine need to do so. The more common reasons for selling are:

- Life circumstances have changed since the time the policy was created. For example, the policy owner may no longer have a beneficiary to which they can leave the money.
- The premiums have become too expensive, either because they increased, or the policy owner had a financial change that made the premium payment a burden.
- The policy owner is looking for a way to convert the resources into money for immediate use.
- The term policy is expiring, and the owner will receive nothing if it does.

What Is the History of the Asset?

The history of life settlements dates back to the 1911 Supreme Court ruling in Grigsby v. Russell. The case involved Dr. Grigsby and the executor of John Burchard's estate, R. L. Russell. In this case, Mr. Burchard was ill and couldn't afford an operation that could potentially save his life. So Mr. Burchard made an agreement with his surgeon, Dr. Grigsby, to exchange ownership of his policy for the operation. A year later, Mr. Burchard passed away, and what followed was court case after court case trying to establish if the transaction was legal. The case finally went to the Supreme Court, where on December 4, 1911, Justice Oliver Wendell Holmes Jr. delivered the majority opinion that created a federal precedent that a life insurance policy is an asset that can be sold:

" . . . life insurance has become in our days one of the best recognized forms of investment and self-compelled saving. So far as reasonable safety permits, it is desirable to give to life policies the ordinary characteristics of property. . . . To deny the right to sell except to persons having such an interest is to diminish appreciably the value of the contract in the owner's hands."[13]

What Are the Current Regulations on Buying and Selling the Asset?

From an investor's perspective, most of the funds that specialize in this asset class require the investor to be accredited. Per the SEC, the definition of an accredited investor is:

A person must have an annual income exceeding $200,000 ($300,000 for joint income) for the last two years with the expectation of earning the same or a higher income in the current year. An individual must have earned income above the thresholds either alone or with a spouse over the last two years. The income test cannot be satisfied by showing one year of an individual's

---

[13] "GRIGSBY v. RUSSELL," FindLaw, https://caselaw.findlaw.com/us-supreme-court/222/149.html.

income and the next two years of joint income with a spouse or has a net worth over $1 million, either alone or together with a spouse (excluding the value of the person's primary residence.[14]

In fact, most of the alternative investments mentioned in this book going forward are geared toward accredited investors. There are exceptions for individual deals, but these rules are in place to protect the investor from unscrupulous characters trying to take advantage of someone that can't afford to lose the money or doesn't know any better. Trust me: These people exist in droves.

In most cases, the fund will source policies directly from a licensed life settlement broker and avoid contact with the seller. This is done very intentionally, as it removes the "boiler room" perception of cold calling seniors asking them if they want to sell their policies. In this arrangement, the sellers usually are the ones who reach out when they have a need.

From a seller's perspective, you should approach selling a life insurance policy very cautiously. Without understanding your options, you may get bad advice from the operator. For example, it's possible that the representative you speak to might not know of the option to reach out to a life insurance broker, or they may falsely give the impression the only option for the policyholder is to surrender the policy or let it lapse.

---

[14] "Accredited Investors - Updated Investor Bulletin," Investor.gov (April 14, 2021), https://www.investor.gov/introduction-investing/general-resources/news-alerts/alerts-bulletins/investor-bulletins/updated-3.

Assuming the policyholder does reach a life settlement broker, the policyholder needs to verify with their state insurance commissioner that the company they are dealing with is properly licensed. The Financial Industry Regulatory Authority (FINRA) recommends doing background checks, verifying registration/license status, and checking for disciplinary history. This can be done through the FINRA BrokerCheck.[15] Finally, keep in mind that the regulations for buying and selling life insurance policies vary by state.

What Is the Market for the Asset?

Life insurance settlements have a pretty robust demand if the criteria are right. As an investor in this space, you have three ways to participate.

Option 1 — Purchase a policy directly through a broker. This is not an ideal starting point since there will be a significant learning curve with broker relationships and understanding the variables. More importantly, brokers might not take you seriously without a significant cash outlay. Remember: Brokers need to know you are serious, and this takes time. Direct purchase should be reserved for experienced investors only.

Option 2 — Make a direct fractional purchase. This takes place when a larger settlement gets broken into smaller pieces for

---

[15] "Seniors beware: What you should know about life settlements," FINRA (July 30, 2009), https://www.finra.org/investors/alerts/seniors-beware-what-you-should-know-about-life-settlements.

investors to divide amongst themselves. This is a better option for new investors, but only if you know the other investors in the deal and find trustworthy underwriting. When new to this space, it might be better to buy a portfolio of a few different fractionalized deals than burn all of your investment capital on one deal.

Option 3 — Invest in a fund. This makes the most sense for a new investor in this space. Just like a fractional purchase, you pool your money with other investors and allow a fund manager to assemble a portfolio of life insurance settlements. This option is better because it gives you instant diversification, and your only major responsibility is vetting the fund manager. While not an easy task, it's only done once, as opposed to vetting every new settlement that comes your way. The only negative is that with most fund models, the investor needs to be accredited and wouldn't be able to participate in the fund without having a third party or accounting/legal professional certify their accredited status. After you do this process once, it usually becomes second nature, but it is a hurdle every time I speak to a new investor. The other nuances are that you would be considered a partner in the fund, which requires a partnership tax return known as a Schedule K. This is done on your behalf by the fund's accountant but it's not unusual for these returns to be filed late, creating a need for filing extensions on your own personal tax returns.

The Bad Apples: Has Anybody Committed Fraud in This Asset Class?
According to the North American Securities Administrators Association (NASAA), viatical settlements are ranked as one of the

top 10 investment scams of all times. There was even a 2011 *American Greed* episode that spotlighted this industry ("The Bling Ring/The Fraudster, The Ex-Stripper and The Missing Millions").

Here is a list of potential red flags that any investor should consider when deciding whether to invest in this space.

1. **Who is handling the money?** — When it comes to investing in life insurance settlements, it's important to know who has access to the funds. If the funds use a reputable third-party custodian (such as a bank) to oversee the money, this adds a layer of protection to the investor's money. If, on the other hand, the funds control the money internally, this can lead to problems down the road if there is any deviation from the original plan.

2. **Are there hidden fees?** — Since a life insurance settlement is a niche alternative asset, there are few standards among the operators, aside from standard operating fees (legal, accounting, etc.). Some operators follow a hedge fund model by charging a placement fee and taking 20% of the ongoing profits. Other fund managers charge a management fee only. As an investor, make sure you compare apples to apples because different fee structures produce very different investment results.

3. **Is there alignment of interests?** — Is the operator personally invested in the fund? In other words, will all parties involved benefit from a positive outcome? If not, this could be a troubling sign.

What Are the Lessons to Be Learned?

There are three key variables to determining the value of a life insurance policy: the remaining life expectancy of the insured, the remaining future premiums, and the total death benefit. Before investing with any operator, speak to them about their philosophy for each variable.

Next, make sure you understand the fund model you are getting involved with. There are life insurance settlement funds that are laser-focused and keep fees small because of their focus and core competency. The simple funds are easy to understand, allowing you to reverse engineer the expected returns. On the other hand, some funds are all over the place and charge huge fees that make it hard to decipher what's going on. You shouldn't need a forensic accountant to figure out the story behind the numbers. I say this *mostly* tongue in cheek; if your investment is high enough, you actually might want to consider hiring a forensic accountant or CPA to audit the company's financials. The company should be willing to provide financial documents, but it is not uncommon for them to require you to sign a non-disclosure agreement (NDA) first. That said, a company refusing to provide the information is a sure sign that they have something to hide and you should walk away from the deal.

> **PRO TIP**: *You may want to reach out to the independent legal professionals involved with the company. Lawyers and accountants have their license to lose if they provide fraudulent information. In essence, this should be part of a thorough due diligence checklist. If you don't know what exactly to put on your checklist, start networking and going to conferences in this space. Find an experienced investor and develop that*

relationship. Note that this shouldn't be a one-sided "pick their brain" extravaganza. Instead, offer value whenever you can and go out of your way to help solve their challenges. Eventually, you will learn how they perform their due diligence, and you'll get a good sense of which operators they trust. That kind of referral goes a long way.

Pros and Cons for the Life Insurance Policy Seller

PROS
- The life settlement payment is typically higher than the cash surrender value of a policy
- The cash payout is usually higher than the accelerated death benefit
- The cash payout can be used however you want
- Provides an "out" for a policy you can't afford

CONS
- Your beneficiaries won't get a payout when you die
- The payout might prevent you from qualifying for Medicaid
- Proceeds from the sale of a policy might be taxed

Pros and Cons for the Life Insurance Policy Investor

PROS
- Relatively unknown niche within a robust industry
- Attractive expected returns
- Credit quality of insurance companies
- Low correlation to other assets
- Investing in a guaranteed life event: death

CONS
- Expected returns can take years to trickle in

- Policy needs to be kept up to date
- Underestimated premiums may cause a capital call— payment of a portion of funds promised by investors
- Negative ethical connotations
- Potentially high investing fees
- Actuary's determination of how long the fund's insured pool will live could be inaccurate, leading to significant investment losses

---

ASK THE EXPERTS: Q&A With Kevin Nichols

Disclaimer: This Q&A is provided for informational purposes only. You should seek your own advice from professional advisors, including lawyers, financial advisors, and accountants, regarding the legal, tax, and financial implications of any investment you contemplate.

Kevin Nichols is a managing partner with Penumbra Capital, which has operated in the life insurance settlement asset class for more than 12 years. They launch their first private equity fund in 2010, and are currently on their 10th fund.

When did you start investing?

In college, primarily in real estate and mutual funds.

How were you introduced to life insurance settlements?

I began investing on a personal level approximately 20 years ago when the only life settlements available were either viaticals or fractional ownership.

What is the biggest negative you discovered?

The biggest negative is the lack of liquidity. Since there is no sophisticated secondary market for life settlements, a potential investor needs to understand that they need to be able to plan on a 10-year term.

What is your most memorable experience in this asset class?

Having policies mature within 3 months of the time that we purchased them. Having investors thank us when the market drops heavily, and their investment is completely unaffected.

What is a common misconception about life insurance settlements?

For many years, the most common misconception was that we were taking advantage of senior citizens. Nothing could be further from the truth. We're actually helping them turn an asset for their beneficiaries into an asset for them to use in their retirement. We never approach seniors to sell their policies. We rely on their financial planners, estate planners, and insurance agents to bring the insureds to us. We always maintain an "arm's length" relationship with the seller.

What is the most important thing an investor should know when considering a life insurance settlement?

Liquidity. Even though most funds will only last eight or nine years, we always advise them to only invest monies that they know that they're not going to need for the next ten years.

What is your professional background, and how did it affect your investing career?

My professional background has always been in finance. From being a bond trader to a financial planner, insurance planner, and financial advisor.

What information sources have been the most influential for you?

Living a Life of Significance *by Joe Jordan*
To Sell Is Human *by Daniel Pink*
Talent Is Overrated *by Geoff Colvin*
Atlas Shrugged *by Ayn Rand*

Who that you personally know do you most respect in business, and why?

That's easy . . . my dad. No better man exists. He always deals with everyone the same way, no matter their net worth or their lot in life.

You are at a holiday party and asked what you do for a living. What do you say?

I manage private equity funds that grow people's money with no market risk and no correlation to the economy. We've never had a single investor lose a single penny in any of our funds.

What is the best piece of investing advice that you've ever received?

"It's hard to get into trouble if you never touch the money."

What's your greatest alternative investment failure, and what would you do differently?

Investing in secured notes. Never rely on someone's promise to pay you back, no matter the apparent collateral.

In five years, do you still see yourself investing in this niche?

Absolutely. Since 1845, no B+ or better American life insurance company has ever failed to pay on a death benefit. I know of no other investment with the absolute guarantees that come with life insurance as an investment.

TAKEAWAYS

- "Trust but verify" is critical in this space due to high fraud
  potential
- Study the space and become more familiar with the three price
  determination variables that help you make an informed
  decision
- Make sure you understand the business model
- Expect to be invested for ten years in this long-term asset
- Network, network, network!

5
APARTMENT BUILDINGS

"Investing in real estate is a lot like handling a loaded gun. Carelessness could end your life; skillful application could save it. Treat it with respect and never ignore the downside scenario."
—Brian Burke, CEO of Praxis Capital

Finally, a chapter that's not about life insurance! I promise that, going forward, the chapters will contain less words like "death" and "life expectancy" and more festive words like "preferred returns," "net operating income" and "internal rate of returns." If you're not smiling now, you will be when you learn their meaning—those words mean serious money to an apartment building investor. Apartment buildings are an alternative investment that I like to call "the gateway investment." That's because once an investor discovers the multi-family space, there's no turning back. Regardless of the background of the investor, it is the fact that the business model repeats so efficiently that resonates with most new investors in this space. It is also the repeatable business plan that creates a very sticky "addict" feeling when you invest in an apartment building. If you've had positive results with a few operators, most likely those operators have other deals in their pipelines in the same areas that are ready for the same business plan that you just witnessed work. Imagine if you found a great CEO with an IPO that was just crushing it—wouldn't you love to invest in another one of their deals? That scenario is unlikely as it would probably take years for that CEO to take another company public (if ever again). But in commercial real estate, you get a chance to keep reinvesting with a successful "CEO" on brand new "IPOs" multiple times per year. How cool is that?

The apartment building industry is extremely diverse and market dependent. It can range from a small landlord who owns a few units, to a Fortune 500 company that operates thousands of units, or "doors," as investors in the space would say. In this chapter, I refer to apartment building investing as the opportunity to purchase into an apartment building syndication passively. This chapter is not meant to explain every nuance of owning an apartment building. My goal is to show you that there's a way of investing in apartment buildings that is within reach for every accredited investor—and even some that are only sophisticated investors.

As an investor, you get to experience the journey from (almost) start to finish. Usually, a deal is presented to an investor after it's in contract, but before acquisition. That means you see the business plan beforehand and get to play your very own round of *Shark Tank* and decide if you like the business plan or not. The more experienced you become, the more you will notice if something doesn't look right.

PRO TIP: *What's critical to understand is that you're not investing in an apartment building; instead, you're investing in a business that has many moving parts, and you need to be able to judge the viability of those moving parts coming together.*

It was when I first invested in a 160-unit apartment building with Matt Faircloth and the Derosa Group in Lexington, KY, that my investing career reached a major turning point. I found myself routinely attending conferences, followed by regular calls with other investors that I had met at these events. It wasn't many at first, but it only took a few connections with the right people to change my trajectory forever. A well-known multi-family operator, Michael Blank, coined a powerful phrase that explains this experience: "the law of the first deal." What Blank meant is that an investor taking on their first successful real estate deal begins to attract the attention of brokers, investors, and other important contacts. For this reason, the second deal is easier than the first, and the third becomes easier still than the second. I always thought the same concept applied to investors in other spaces within the investing community too. For me, investing in my first deal gave me motivation to attend two events: The MidAtlantic Real Estate Investor Summit hosted by veteran investor Dave Van Horn, and the relaunch of The Renault Winery Resort hosted by entrepreneur, investor, and business owner Josh McCallen. Both events allowed me to connect with two of my future partners. From there, I joined masterminds, invested in various asset classes, started an investment club, and put in multi-million-dollar offers to purchase my own apartment buildings—all of which eventually culminated in the founding of SIH Capital Group (and the writing of this book!). But if I rewind everything to one moment, it was that first investment in the Lexington apartment building that jolted me into action.

What Is the Asset?

At its core, apartment buildings provide a tenant with a place to live in exchange for a monthly rent payment. In order to purchase the apartment building, an operator (otherwise known as a general partner) pools together funds from various investors (otherwise known as limited partners[16]), and then secures a loan for the remaining balance. This process is called a syndication, and it allows an investor to buy into a larger deal for a nominal amount compared to the total purchase. In most of the deals I have seen, the minimum investment was set to $50,000. This might seem like a lot of money, but the $50,000 allows you to buy into a property that is worth millions and receive all of the benefits that a larger business provides. For example, one of my previous investments of $50,000 gave me a small share of a $70,000,000 complex.

Let's compare this investment to the single-family property I once owned in East Orange, NJ, (discussed in Chapter 1), which had a similar market value of $50,000. With the syndication, I had professional property management, consistent rental distributions, better and less leveraged terms on a non-recourse mortgage, and operational efficiencies of 700 units, all with a professional team of operators executing on a clear business plan with a well-defined exit. On my single-family, I had to manage the property myself because the cash flow wasn't good enough to pay for property management, I received rent haphazardly, and since I only had one tenant, I received zero benefits from scale. The mortgage rates were also worse, and I had to personally guarantee my loan. Plus, I had no idea when I would be able to sell because that was dependent on the market for other single-family homes

---

[16] Limited partners also get the benefits of limited liability with practically no recourse if the investment goes bad. There is a common saying that a limited partner can only lose their entire investment, but no more.

in the area—and it was moving slow. Are you starting to see the difference?

Now let's talk about appreciation. Unlike the residential world, where a house's price is largely determined by the selling price of a similar house next door, the value of an apartment building is based on the net operating income (NOI) of the building and the capitalization rate. Both terms may seem foreign, but they are actually quite simple. The NOI is a formula used to show how profitable a property is by subtracting all of the reasonably necessary operating expenses from all of the revenue it produces. The capitalization rate is a gauge of what the market is willing to pay for that profitability. Knowing those two items allows the apartment building operator to create a plan that can increase the NOI. For example, an operator might notice that there are three apartment buildings in exactly the same condition within a two-mile range of each other. Each respective tenant has access to the same great school district, low neighborhood crime rates, and all of the same amenities, except one of the buildings doesn't have a dog park. At the building without the dog park, there are fewer tenants paying a pet fee, and the average rent is $100 less. It might not seem like much, but when we look at an extra $100 a month across 100+ units across a 12-month period, the NOI adds up quickly. That's the magic of scale.

The operator may want to come up with a post-acquisition plan for installing a new dog park and, at the same time, enforce the pet fee rules that had been lax with the previous property management. The result? The NOI increases, and the property becomes more valuable (assuming that the cap rate remains constant), and the investors participate in some of that upside.

When the capitalization rate is low, as it is in today's market (meaning investors are willing to pay a lot for a low amount of profitability), the business plan usually needs to involve multiple plans of actions, such as making exterior updates, catching up on deferred maintenance, making cosmetic interior upgrades, and seeking other ways to add value to the tenants' lives that warrants a rent increase. Since rent increases and expense decreases are the biggest drivers of increasing NOI, the focus of the business plan should clearly demonstrate how it directly correlates to some combination of the two.

The benefit to a low capitalization rate market is that if the operator is successful at increasing the NOI of the apartment building, that increase is worth more to the next buyer because the market is paying a higher multiple for profitability.

EXAMPLE
Property Value = NOI/Cap Rate

A $100,000 increase in NOI at a 4-cap rate increases a property's value by $2.5 million:

BEFORE: $10,000,000 = $400,000/4%
AFTER: $12,500,00 = $500,000/4%

At a 5-cap rate, the value of the property only increases by $2 million:

BEFORE: $8,000,000 = $400,000/5%
AFTER: $10,000,000 = $500,000/5%

After the 2007–2009 recession, in most residential markets, where income and population were both increasing, there was a steady compression of cap rates in the apartment building space. This created a significant tailwind for any operator during this time period because someone would just come along and pay a higher multiple for the same profits. Today, operators do not have the same luxury, as cap rates are expected to rise from today's levels.

This is important because part of your job as an investor is to evaluate any business plan in the context of where the cap rate will be when you need to sell the property (typically three to seven years). The business plan provides pro forma financial statements that project what returns the investor can expect to see and when. It also lays out the action items needed to raise the NOI, as well as the operator's opinion on where the cap rate is going. Since neither you nor the operator is likely a PhD economist, what you are looking for is consistency. If you evaluate ten deals, and nine of those deals project an increase in the cap rate but lower overall returns, and one projects a higher overall return but with a flat or decreasing cap rate, one has to question the higher returns. The decreasing cap rates may actually be accurate because the operator secured an incredibly favorable price on the purchase and expects to receive the market rate when they sell, but most likely it's a sign that the operator is inexperienced or willing to overpromise to get the deal done. Either way, you should be aware of the general consensus for operators in that market.

We learned how an apartment building is valued and how its appreciation can be increased by a well-thought-out business plan. Now, let's discuss income. In the world of stocks, if your company is profitable, management may choose to pay shareholder dividends or reinvest in the company. An apartment building works exactly the same way. During the early years of acquisition, the general partner may choose to hold onto extra reserves and reinvest some additional money into the building if they feel it would produce a better overall return for investors. Usually, the renovation money (known as "capital expenditures" or "capex") is raised up front, so profits can be distributed on a monthly or quarterly basis from ongoing operations. I have seen situations where the operators raised enough money to renovate a portion of the units during the initial takeover, but the amount of rent collected for those units far exceeded the original business plan. In this case, the operator can choose to reinvest in more units rather than pay distributions in order to increase the NOI faster, which, in turn, creates a higher return for investors. But, in general, operators try to stick to their business plan as much as possible.

As the plan progresses, the distributions should increase over time since the property should be more profitable. While on the subject of distributions, we should mention what a *preferred return* is. A preferred return is the hurdle that an investor needs to see in distributions before the investor starts splitting the profits with the operator. Preferred distributions tend to range from 6%–8%— meaning the first 6–8% of the profits is designated to the investor. If the preferred distributions are not met for a specific quarter, then the difference is supposed to accrue until the investor sees their full preferred distributions. Preferred distributions are meant to protect investors, but there are some caveats:

- Watch for language that indicates that the preferred return only accrues for a set period of time instead of over the life of the deal.

- Some operators have a strong following and can raise money without providing a preferred return. This may indicate a very strong track record.

During the holding period, any distributions made to a limited partner would be very tax friendly due to the enormous depreciation an apartment building creates annually. There is also a term called *cost segregation* that supercharges the depreciation an investor sees on their Schedule K. In simple terms, the investor may have received their share of the distributions, but the investor document may show a negative number because the depreciation share for the investor was greater than the distribution received. However, taxes on those distributions are only deferred until the property sells, at which time, you may need to pay them. The key is to plan and know that these gains are not tax free indefinitely. On a related note, most operators do a great job of expediting Schedule Ks for their investors, but if they are late, you'll need to file a tax extension.

When the property sells, the cumulative distributions paid to the investors during all of the years of holding the property—including any profits from the sale—get adjusted for the value of time, and the end result is your internal rate of return (IRR). This is the primary means of comparing two deals side by side since no two deals are identical. If a deal is able to produce the same total returns in three years that it does in five years, the IRR will be significantly higher because that money is returned to the investor quicker and can be placed into another deal that much sooner. This concept of the "time value of money" (TVM) is also why some operators try to refinance during the hold period to return investors some of their original investment. This can only be done if the value of the property has increased, which leaves less money in the deal for the investor while keeping their existing equity in place because the refinance involves adding debt, not decreasing equity. When this occurs, the cash flow is less in the aftermath, but the IRR% increases substantially because investors can compound their returned money into other deals. Earlier, we discussed an operator choosing not to distribute regular distributions in order to more aggressively implement their business plan; the refinance or early sale of a property is precisely why you would do that. The shorter the hold or the less investor capital left in the deal, the greater the IRR% is when the asset is performing. TVM is a very real consideration in the apartment building world. In many ways, it is the single most important metric an operator gets judged on.

We've covered a lot of ground. Let's do a quick review:

We know an operator puts a deal together and is usually referred to as a general partner; you can think of them as the CEO. An investor is commonly referred to as a limited partner; you can think of them as the common stock shareholder. The limited partner is presented with a business plan on how the operator plans to increase the NOI and create value for the investor. If the investor likes the plan, they invest alongside other investors in a syndication. After the building is acquired, the investor may receive dividend-like payments called distributions, and those are usually paid monthly or quarterly. At the end of the investment, the NOI hopefully is considerably higher and, depending how the cap rates moved during the holding period, the value of the building should be higher. When sold, profits are returned back to the investors, first starting with any unpaid preferred returns and then split per the operating agreement. The total returns are then weighted by the value of time, and you are left with the IRR% of the deal. While I used the word "hopefully" multiple times here, keep in mind that hold times are like moving goal posts. This is the operator's profession and livelihood, and they are constantly getting brokers' opinions on the value of their properties. Given the significance of the time value of money, there's nothing stopping the operators from selling earlier if the cap rates compress on them, or if they execute on their plan faster than expected—just like there's nothing stopping them from increasing the hold time (if proper financing is in place) if the cap rates increase more than expected, or there's significant setbacks to the business plan. In the end, you're investing in the operator and their ability to manage this multimillion-dollar business. Not much different than stocks if you think about it that way, except stocks get repriced daily, whereas in real estate, the cap rates reprice gradually over time in a much less volatile fashion.

What Is the History of the Asset?

Investing in apartment buildings is nothing new. Apartment buildings themselves can be traced back to Roman times with buildings called *insulas*, which were similar to what we call a mixed-use building today, where there is a shop on the ground floor and six or seven floors of living space above. Ironically, due to safety concerns and the requirement for climbing extra stairs (since there were obviously no elevators), the higher apartments with the better views were the cheapest. In Paris, apartment buildings began showing up in the 18th century, with a similar price reduction for apartments located on the higher floors. And in New York City, the early 19th century saw the rise of tenements that tried to accommodate a population that was doubling every ten years for a better part of the century. By the turn of the century, almost 2/3 of New York City's residents lived in an apartment building.[17]

Fast forward to today: There are over 108.5 million renters in America,[18] and that number is increasing yearly. There are numerous reasons why the number keeps growing—from people getting married later in life, to starting families later, and having more college loan debt. For these reasons, apartments located in the right market have a huge tailwind at their back. There is just not enough supply to meet the ever-growing demand.

Investing in apartment buildings was very much a private club affair up until the Jumpstart Our Business Startups (JOBS) Act passed in 2012. Previously, anyone could theoretically have purchased their own apartment building with their own funds, but operators were constrained from making general solicitations of investors, making the transactions very private within operators' own immediate circle. It only made sense for the operators to target the wealthiest among their immediate networks, and the result was that investing in apartment buildings was an exclusive club that only well-connected individuals belonged to.

That all changed with the passing of the JOBS Act, which overturned restrictions that were in place for the 80 years prior.

---

[17] Alice Bradley, "A brief history of the apartment," REA Group (July 12, 2016), https://www.realestate.com.au/news/brief-history-apartment-living/.

[18] Alcynna Lloyd, "Decade in review: Number of U.S. renters surpasses 100 million," HousingWire (March 12, 2020), https://www.housingwire.com/articles/decade-in-review-number-of-u-s-renters-surpasses-100-million/.

Special rules were written by the SEC allowing non-accredited investors to now invest in private transactions. In addition, general solicitation was now available to attract accredited investors that were not in the sponsor's immediate network. The cumulative effects of the new rules meant that the doors to this exclusive niche of operators and their inner circles of investors were blown wide open.

All of a sudden, scores of podcasts, books, webinars, and other educational materials flooded the internet to build awareness for investing in commercial real estate. With that came a wave of amateur operators beginning to take on deals that quite frankly were over their heads. Most were able to profit with an extremely strong market on their side. Others were not as fortunate, but because they were limited partners, they had very little recourse against the operators.

The good news is that the apartment investing industry has not looked back since, and there have never been more options for operators and investors, whether accredited or not. Looking at what has transpired in the industry since the passing of the JOBS Act, I think it's safe to safe that it is one of the most significant laws to be passed in our century for passive investors. Of course, there have certainly been some cautionary tales along the way, some of which I will cover later in this chapter.

What Are the Current Regulations on Buying and Selling the Asset?

There are a few key regulations that an investor needs to be aware of. First, it's important to understand that when you invest in an apartment building as a limited partner, your investment in the building is a security. The opportunity to purchase the security is called the offering, which is supposed to outline all the risks associated with investing in that security. This process is governed by Regulation D of the federal securities laws. In order to comply with Regulation D, the operator and their securities lawyer must file a 506(b) or a 506(c) exemption.

The biggest pro to an operator using a 506I exemption is that it allows them to advertise to investors for their offering. However, the operator has to take *reasonable steps to verify* the investor's accredited status. This means using third-party verification, such as a certified accountant, licensed lawyer, or a professional service like Verify Investor for every prospective investor. This also means that if you are not accredited, you won't be eligible to invest—but there are 506(b) exemptions you might qualify for.

An operator that uses the 506(b) exemption can't advertise their deals, but they can accept both accredited and non-accredited investors. They can also accept an investor's claim of being accredited without being required to verify their status. The catch is that the investor has to have a pre-existing relationship with the operator prior to the offering going live. That pre-existing relationship can consist of a combination of a questionnaire, email exchanges, and phone conversations for a duration that is long enough for the operator to clearly establish that the investor is suitable for this investment. The golden rule is three touches, but different securities attorneys will give you different variations of this rule.

A word of caution: Before considering any investment, you should know if you meet the requirements of being an accredited investor because you don't want to waste anyone's time, including your own. There is no loophole for investing in a 506l offering if you are not. If you are on the cusp of being accredited, it might make sense to add 506l operators to your prospect list. Just be honest about your timeline with any operators that you are looking to establish relationships with.

What Is the Market for the Asset?

In terms of selling your investment, there are very few options. In fact, a typical offering states that there will most likely not be a secondary market for this security, and you should not invest if you have a need for this money prior to the intended hold period. That being said, some operators will purchase back shares at a discount—sometimes as high as 20%. There are also third-party companies that attempt to provide liquidity for these types of events, but they typically broker larger deals.

Reminder: This lack of liquidity is one of the reasons why I think apartment building syndications are such a great complement to equities. Your equity portfolio is liquid at all times, which comes with a fair share of volatility. But limited partnership shares are extremely hard to sell, and an operator is not going to sell a building mid-business-plan just because of a debt crisis in a foreign country or any other reason why the stock market decides to sell off 10% or more. The end result is a very stable asset that moves primarily based on the NOI.

The Bad Apples: Has Anybody Committed Fraud in This Asset Class?

Unfortunately, yes. If you Google "fraud" and "Ponzi schemes," real estate deals come up frequently. This is why investing in alternative investments is termed a very "active passive investment." Yes, the actual investment is very passive, but the amount of work that goes into networking, learning about the investment, and conducting due diligence beforehand is anything but passive.

As a lesson, let's take a look at one of my worst investments.

While it wasn't fraud, it was definitely a case of a bad apple. After the JOBS Act passed, there was a mad rush of online crowdfunding platforms and new operators masquerading as real estate experts. Sadly, a lot of investors bought into what they were selling at the time. Unfortunately, I was one of those investors. In 2018, I found and invested in a crowdfunding platform that promised vigorous due diligence and cited a deal rejection rate of 99%, claiming that none of their deals had lost principal. Plus, their minimum required investments were 5x lower than investing directly with an operator. While that combination was too good for me to pass up at the time, the phrase "you get what you pay for" now comes to mind as I type these words. I was an easy mark at that time: I didn't know what I didn't know, and I was blinded by the promised returns. Little did I know that the platform was just too new to have lost principal, and an avalanche of losers were about to hit.

The platform had also introduced a complicated middleman legal entity, which meant that I was investing in the platform's LLC and not the actual operator. When things got bad, the operator refused to even talk to me. While it was extremely unprofessional, it was within their rights because of the agreement they had with the investing platform. In addition, when I had a deal exit, I had to wait for the operator to close their books and then the investing platform's LLC to close their books, essentially doubling the period in which I received no interest on my capital.

One call with an experienced investor would have set me straight, but I was only a passive investor at that time, and I wasn't networking. Shortly after I invested, the real estate platform failed to secure a round of venture capital funding and collapsed. No real estate investor should ever have to say that their real estate investment depended on venture capital financing. If you do, you did something very wrong.

Luckily, most of the investing platforms that had bad business models like that one are now out of business. Honestly, there are a few remaining that I would still recommend now, but generally speaking, going directly to a platform to avoid putting in the work to network, perform due diligence, and learn the industry is a huge mistake.

The saddest part of this story is that I followed a few investor forums that got burned from the same platform. First-time accredited investors lost a huge amount of money in this platform's "highly selective" investments. At the time, I tried to create groups in which we could share ongoing investments in this space, but the damage was already done. A majority of those investors will never invest in another syndication again, and they actively warn others about how dangerous and speculative it is to invest in syndication.

Tax Considerations

Real estate—specifically, investments in syndications—are considered tax-friendly assets. What exactly does that mean? When considering a syndication, you'll find that operators use buzzwords like "tax efficiency," "pass-through depreciation," and "tax deferral." In reality, investing in syndications requires considerable proper due diligence and tax planning if you want to take advantage of all those buzzwords that have become clichés in this space. Prior to investing in any potential deal, you should discuss your options with your accountant, who can explain everything from whether or not to purchase the investment in a retirement account (which is done easily and often these days), to how to invest in a way in which passive gains will be offset by passive losses in a non-retirement account. Operators are often willing to send you a sample Schedule K of a previous deal so you can show your accountant for estimation purposes.

The best piece of advice I received when talking to multiple real estate CPAs is that investing in syndications is not magic—contrary to some operators' statements. All it does is kick the "tax can" down the road. With proper planning, you may be able to keep kicking that can down the road even until death, but make no mistake—it's not as simple as it's made to look by some operators.

Keep in mind that your current accountant may not have enough real estate experience to properly answer your questions. This is where networking with other investors is critical. While it's considered taboo to talk about how much money you make with your current network, talking about tax planning with other real estate investors is welcomed. Weird, I know—but your network can help you learn more about current tax strategies and also gain referrals to other qualified CPAs.

Leveraging Your Network to Buy Smarter

Investing in apartment buildings is not cheap; investing in your network shouldn't be, either. Throughout my investing career, a dollar spent on networking has saved me hundreds of dollars of potentially bad/fraudulent/disastrous investments. In fact, I am such a proponent of networking with other investors that if this is a deal breaker for you, I would advise you not to invest in alternative investments. Alternative niche assets like these are not covered by scores of Wall Street analysts, and many times, other investors are your *only* source for current relevant information.

One prominent syndicator, Joe Fairless, and his co-author Theo Hicks wrote in their *Best Ever Apartment Syndication Book* about the obligation that current investors and operators have to educate non-investors about this space—comparing it to an apocalypse where only you have the cure, and you have to convince everyone else that it is the *actual* cure. People's natural tendencies will be to doubt you, and you have to overcome that doubt to convince them and save society. While this metaphor may be over the top, I still remember it vividly to this day, and it reminds me of the bigger picture of *helping* and not *selling* when I speak to potential investors. At the end of the day, if I believe that investing privately in apartment buildings is a better alternative than real estate investment trusts (REITS) that trade on Wall Street, shouldn't I try to help other investors by showing them that there is an alternative?

Another networking tip that helped me when I was starting out in syndications was creating a small investment club. Mine was with two other like-minded accredited investors. We discussed partnering on some of the syndications we were individually thinking about. This way, we would split the minimum investment and get some diversification at the same time. After six months of preparation, we all agreed to form one investment LLC with our own operating agreement. During due diligence, we learned that all three of us would have to be actively involved in the decisions of the LLC. Otherwise, if one of us went passive, we would need to create our own securities offering outlining all of the risks to our one passive investor. It's also incredibly important that everyone in the LLC is accredited; otherwise, the LLC won't be able to invest in 506I offerings, which are the majority of current offerings.

Having two partners to look over each deal helped me significantly. We diversified with three different operators in three different markets for the same investment one of us would have made in one deal. Looking back at significant life events, this was one of them. Our collective learning curve exponentially grew going forward because we learned as a team to ask the right questions.

A word of caution: If you go this route, designate one person in the LLC to be the dedicated liaison for each investment. The goal is to treat the investment entity as a singular entity with one point of contact. Just like operators can be labeled as difficult to work with, so can investors. Operators communicate with each other, and if you have multiple investors reaching out to them from the same entity, it can feel unprofessional, diminish your reputation, and get confusing very quickly.

In Chapter 14, I'll share some additional best practices for building out your network.

What Are the Lessons to Be Learned?

Once you start building your network and invest in a few deals that perform well, it becomes intoxicating. When a business plan gets executed perfectly, the feeling that this asset is too good to be true can take hold. But if the business plan doesn't go as planned, it's time to learn why. The failures are far and away your best investments when starting out, as long as you don't repeat the same mistakes. Here are some pointers to keep in mind:

- Run a Google check and formal background check on a prospective operator; both are easier and faster than you think.
- Use a due diligence checklist. (There is an excellent one in *The Hands-Off Investor: An Insider's Guide to Investing in Passive Real Estate Syndications* by Brian Burke.)
- Ask your network who the best operators are that they have invested in, and why.
- Ask an operator to put you on their communication list for a specific deal prior to investing. (This might be a stretch, but it can go a long way in building a relationship if they agree to it.)
- Listen to as many podcasts as possible that feature a prospective operator. You can tell a lot by the way they answer certain questions and the information that they are willing to share.
- Don't invest all at once. You learn after every deal you invest in, so it pays to space them out.
- Diversify both your markets and operators (no matter how much you may love operators you've worked with in the past).

- If you choose to invest in a crowdfunding platform, exercise caution: Make sure your investment is with the operator and that you will have an open line of communication with them.
- Join investment clubs. There are at least three well-known investment clubs that exclusively focus on syndications. These clubs are created by investors for investors, and the knowledge they share is gold.

Note: If you eventually want to become an operator yourself, there's no better way to learn best practices than investing as a limited partner in a few different deals. Just be careful that the operator you choose to invest in is actually experienced. You won't be able to sniff out a true amateur for some time, and the worst thing you can do is build up a portfolio of such deals. Be patient; it will come to you.

The Pros and Cons of Apartment Building Investing
PROS
- Instant scale
- Professional management
- Completely passive if you are a limited partner
- Tax deferral
- Great way to learn

CONS
- Proliferation of amateur operators
- Added layer of tax planning
- Extensions may be needed for tax returns
- Capital calls
- Very limited recourse for a bad operator
- Very illiquid market for a limited partner

ASK THE EXPERTS: Q&A With Brian Burke

Disclaimer: This Q&A is provided for informational purposes only. You should seek your own advice from professional advisors, including lawyers, financial advisors, and accountants, regarding the legal, tax, and financial implications of any investment you contemplate.

Brian Burke is President/CEO of Praxis Capital Inc., a vertically integrated real estate private equity investment firm. Brian has acquired over half a billion dollars' worth of real estate over a 30-year career including over 3,000 multi-family units and more than 700 single-family homes, with the assistance of proprietary software that he wrote himself. Brian has subdivided land, built homes, and constructed self-storage, but really prefers to reposition existing multi-family properties. Brian is the author of The Hands-Off Investor: An Insider's Guide to Investing in Passive Real Estate Syndications *and is a frequent public speaker at real estate conferences and events nationwide.*

When did you start investing?

1989 in a single-family home; 2002 in multi-family.

How were you introduced to apartment building investments?

I had one rental house and one rental condo that I wanted to 1031 exchange into something larger. I didn't know anything about commercial real estate or apartments, but I had a real estate agent who was selling all of my flip homes that was a CCIM—which is a professional designation of commercial real estate brokers. I asked him about how to analyze commercial real estate. He sat me down in his office for a couple of hours and showed me the ropes. About a month later, he got a listing for a 16-unit apartment building. I looked at it, ran the numbers, and it seemed to be exactly what I was looking for. I made an offer, which included my 1031 exchange funds, a loan from a bank, and a 10% seller carryback, and the seller accepted! I think that having the broker on both sides of the deal really made a difference. Had I not had that, the seller probably wouldn't have taken me seriously. I ended up owning that property for over 15 years, and it was a great way to learn the business. Big enough to learn, but small enough that a problem wouldn't wipe me out.

What is the biggest negative you discovered?

It's a capital-intensive business. The larger the property, the more money it takes to acquire and operate it. If you are an individual investor utilizing your own funds, you'll find that your ability to grow your portfolio declines rapidly unless you have a lot of capital to begin with. In the beginning, I was really stretching myself thin as I grew my portfolio but felt that it was what I had to do to get the asset base and experience. That paid off because it gave me the track record needed to raise money from others and exponentially propel my growth. Had I not gone through with the investments I made, even though they were a stretch for me, I wouldn't be where I am today.

What is your most memorable experience in this asset class?

It was a property I bought shortly after the real estate collapse of 2006–2007 and just before the economic collapse of 2008–2009. I *got the property up to about 99% occupancy, and then suddenly the bottom fell out of the economy. I used to say that "half of the units are empty, and the other half aren't paying." That was a bit of an exaggeration, but not that far off. I ended up making the $15,000 per month mortgage payment out of my own pocket for over three years just so I could protect my investor's investment. It was a painful experience, but a tremendous lesson. I was fortunate to have sold that asset several years later for a profit, and even got all of my money back and a positive return for my investors—quite an accomplishment when many people in a similar situation were losing their apartment buildings to foreclosure.*

What is a common misconception about apartment building investments?

That "everybody needs a place to live," a common statement that I hear investors repeat when they are trying to convince their investors that multi-family is a recession-proof investment. I can tell you from personal experience—it may be recession-resistant, but it's not recession-proof. The truth is that everyone does, in fact, need a place to live, but there's no guarantee that place will be in one of your apartments. When people lose their job, they might go back to live with their parents, move in with friends or other relatives, or double-up with a roommate. But they won't be renting your apartment. It's important to plan for economic cycles and underwrite for periods of higher vacancy and larger bad debt losses.

What is the most important thing an investor should know when considering an apartment building investment?

In aviation, there is a thing called the "accident chain." Airplane crashes don't happen because of one "biggest thing." Instead, a series of small missteps happen in sequence until disaster strikes. If any one of the small missteps didn't occur, the accident chain is broken, and no disaster occurs. Investing in real estate works in a similar way: There isn't a single "gotcha." Instead, there are a myriad of little things, that, if they all add up correctly, can result in an outstanding investment. Or one or more of the little things can go wrong, resulting in a satisfying investment. Or all of the little things can misalign, resulting in an investment disaster.

What is your professional background, and how did it affect your investing career?

In my early investing years, I worked in law enforcement. I worked the swing shift with Monday, Tuesday, and Wednesday off. This meant that I had nearly the entire business week off except after 4 p.m. on Thursday and Friday, leaving me plenty of time to manage my real estate investing business. The other benefit came when I set out to raise money from investors. Naturally, their biggest fear is that they'll lose their money, and one of the ways to lose money is if I were to take it and disappear. My law enforcement background went a long way toward gaining people's trust. They knew that if I could pass the agency's background checks, I probably wasn't a crook.

What information sources have been the most influential for you?

Aside from my own book, of course—The Hands-Off Investor [laughing]—in the early years, Rich Dad Poor Dad was a book that taught me to think of the "why." The book The Secret made me aware of the power of visualizing your dreams and manifesting them into reality. Books on Microsoft Access, Excel, and Visual Basic taught me how to write my own databases, software, and spreadsheets, which turned out to be enormously valuable in my business and growth. I didn't even know it at the time, but having the tools I created put us in a different league in the eyes of investors and partners.

Who that you personally know do you most respect in business, and why?

I'm going to go off the script here and say my wife. Not just because she's put up with me for over 30 years, but also because all of the deals that I've regretted match up pretty cleanly with the list of deals she suggested that I not do. I guess that means that her sixth sense is better than mine, or it just means that I should listen to my wife. But what earns real respect is that even though she said, "Don't do it," and I did it anyway (while justifying all of the reasons why this "deal is great"), she stuck by me through the ups, downs, and failures. Maybe that means that she's really good at seeing a value-add deal because life is pretty good now, and giving up early would have meant missing out on where we are today.

You are at a holiday party and asked what you do for a living. What do you say?

I manage a private investment fund. Since I don't hustle for money at holiday parties, the conversation usually moves to the next topic shortly after that statement. Unless, of course, they just happen to be in the market for some new investments—in which case they are free to ask—but that rarely happens.

What is the best piece of investing advice that you've ever received?

I once asked Maxwell Drever, a legend in the industry, what was the biggest thing that changed the course of his investment business. "The institutions," he said. Having them invest with him was the flame that lit the fuse.

What's your greatest alternative investment failure, and what would you do differently?

My greatest failure was also my most memorable experience (see answer above). Funny thing—you can forget the successes, but the failures stick with you, and the scars heal slowly. Even though I ultimately had a good enough outcome, the experience was painful while I was in the thick of it, and that pain resulted in me rethinking the way I approached commercial real estate underwriting. No longer do I lack respect for the power of adverse economic cycles; instead, I now plan for them. I am very careful about the terms of the debt on a property, underwrite to adverse economic vacancy, and perform multiple sensitivity analyses. Back when all of this happened, I didn't understand any of that.

In five years, do you still see yourself investing in this niche?

As long as the fundamentals of the strategy continue to support it, yes. But I've done just about everything there is to do in real estate, so if the opportunity shifts elsewhere, I'm well equipped to pivot. Hopefully, I still have a good 20 years left in me. That would make it a 50-year career. Sounds fulfilling, doesn't it?

ASK THE EXPERTS: Q&A With Andrew Cushman

Disclaimer: This Q&A is provided for informational purposes only. You should seek your own advice from professional advisors, including lawyers, financial advisors, and accountants, regarding the legal, tax, and financial implications of any investment you contemplate.

Andrew Cushman is Principal of Vantage Point Acquisitions. For over a decade, Andrew has been growing real estate investment businesses full-time. In total, Andrew and his team have acquired and repositioned over 2,100 multi-family units to date. Outside of the business world, Andrew is a certified alpine ski instructor who also enjoys surfing and trying to not be outwitted by his two children.

When did you start investing?

The first investment I made was in 2004. I "house hacked" (before such a term existed) my primary residence when I bought my condo and rented out the second bedroom to a guy I knew. His rent just barely paid the mortgage. That was eye opening. My first actual investment property was purchased in 2007.

How were you introduced to apartment building investments?

My wife and I were flipping houses full time, and things were going great. In total, we completed 27 single-family flips, all of which were very profitable. But we saw that the market was going to shift, and apartment buildings would directly benefit from that shift. With all the foreclosures in the Great Recession, the housing market came to a halt. It was hard to qualify for a loan and we were due for an expansion once we came out of the recession. Those two things sound like positives for apartments. We came to our mentor for single family flips, and asked him if he knew someone we could learn apartments from. He introduced me to guy who had done about 800 units. We hired him as a mentor, and in 2011, he guided us through our first acquisition of a mostly vacant 92-unit property on the other side of the country. That first property was eventually sold for several times its original purchase price, and now we acquire Class B, value-add properties throughout the Southeast.

What was the biggest negative you discovered?

There are so many things now that I'm aware of that we did on our first deal that we'd never do again. One thing that we discovered after getting into a contract for our first apartment building was how hard it was to raise money at that time. In 2011, most people were still scared of real estate and not having done it yet and not having a big enough network at that time would have made me more cautious in hindsight. In time, we also learned that it's very *easy to underestimate repairs and you have to pay attention to key market data, such as median income and crime levels.*

What is your most memorable experience in this asset class?

That's a tough one. I would say finally getting enough money to close that first apartment building. I remember, I was on a family vacation. I just had a conference call with three investors, and they agreed to invest the rest of the money I needed to finish the raise for that very first deal. That was memorable. It took me six months to raise $1.2 million.

The most memorable recent experience was that my company just raised $12 million in 28 hours. I had no idea that demand was so strong.

What is a common misconception about apartment building investments?

There's quite a few. From an operator's perspective, people mistakenly believe that, like single family properties, you have to personally qualify for a loan. If you try to buy anything four units or less, then you have to go to a residential mortgage lender and have them qualify you for that loan by taking a really deep look at you and your financial situation. That's not true once you get to apartments and commercial. For anything above five units, the lender is not really focused on you; the bank will make sure that you have some liquid net worth, but really, they're underwriting the property. A lot of people think that their personal credit score would stop them from getting into apartments. In reality, that not something that's heavily weighted.

Separately, the biggest mistakes I see operators make is going into a deal undercapitalized and not bringing enough extra cash upfront to cover unforeseen capital and operating expenses.

From an investor perspective, I receive a lot of questions regarding the deal structure. Who gets paid, when, and how? How does depreciation work in syndications? In general, depreciation and all the ways that it can benefit the investor are commonly misunderstood. Number one, they don't think as limited partners that they will receive depreciation. And two, they don't realize that the income from the investment in the apartments will probably be tax free until it's sold. In many cases, with proper tax planning, any excess depreciation can be used to shelter other income.

What is the most important thing an investor should know when considering an apartment building investment?

A bad operator can take an amazing deal and make it into a terrible deal, while a really good operator can take a bad deal and at least save it. At the end of the day, the deal is important, but the operator and their skill and integrity are more important.

If you're looking at investing as a limited partner, some of the questions you should absolutely consider are: 1) What are the market rent growth assumptions? 2) What kind of capitalization rate expansion is expected, and will it change over the life of the investment? 3) What kind of insurance will be placed on the property in terms of valuation and deductible? (There are lots of people who get high deductible insurance for a cheaper premium, but then something happens, and they have to get money from investors to cover the capital.) 4) What levels of reserves are needed, both for capital and operation?

What is your professional background, and how did it affect your investing career?

Before getting into real estate, I was a chemical engineer. While not directly related, it certainly helped with building the right mindset. As an engineer, you receive valuable experience with analyzing data, logical thinking, and cost-benefit analysis, which all come in handy when analyzing apartment buildings. In regard to decision-making, you learn to put a heavy emphasis on numbers and analysis, rather than excitement, fear, or any other emotion.

What information sources have been the most influential for you?

Multi-Family Millions *and* Emerging Real Estate Markets *by David Lindahl*
How to Win Friends and Influence People *by Dale Carnegie*
Start with No *by Jim Camp*
Never Split the Difference *by Chris Voss*
BiggerPockets *podcast*
Macro Voice *podcast*
Bisnow *newsletter*

I would also include my networking groups. I am in Gobundance, and while that's not a multi-family mastermind, just being around those guys helped me learn and grow and expand my mindset over the years. And then I am in a multi-unit apartment-focused mastermind. It's not a paid thing; eight of us just get together once a month. That group is a tremendous resource of information in terms of what other operators are doing in the market, what they're seeing, what they're experiencing. That's definitely important information, in terms of mechanics, operating, and mindset.

Who that you personally know do you most respect in business, and why?

While a handful of people come to mind for different reasons, my original mentor Mike Ballard is someone I admire. He's been doing this for 15 years and has done 3,500 units. Every time I talk to somebody in the real estate world who knows Mike, they have nothing but good things to say. As long as I have known him, he's always been the same high integrity guy, cares about other people, does good deals, and is good at business. I have a lot of respect for him.

Also, I'm friends with Michael Becker, a syndicator in Dallas. I have a ton of respect for him because even though he had some advantages with his commercial background, once he decided to go into apartments, he just blew it away. He's built a massive investment base with over 10,000 units in around six years.

You are at a holiday party and asked what you do for a living. What do you say?

It depends on how much time I have and my sense of the person that I am speaking with. I say something like if you want to go on a cruise in the Caribbean, you don't go buy a $2 billion ship, and then try to learn how to navigate around. What you do is put together a bunch of people and pool together their money. Then, everybody gets to go on this ship and share in the benefits of it without having to buy it themselves. That's basically what I do. I provide the benefits of passive income to people looking to diversify with passive income streams by putting together investment opportunities that most people wouldn't have access to otherwise.

What is the best piece of investing advice that you've ever received?

Don't buy in low-income, high-crime areas—the more important part being the crime, but generally, the two attributes go hand in hand.

What's your greatest alternative investment failure, and what would you do differently?

In the beginning, we didn't have all the necessary systems in place, including a refined screening process. I think it was our third deal where we accidentally bought a deal in a low-income, high-crime area. Fortunately, we did not syndicate that deal, which turned out to be a blessing. We lost money on it when we sold, but we got to move on to a better deal.

In five years, do you still see yourself investing in this niche?

I do. We enjoy the business. I believe it has very strong long-term trends and fundamentals that will continue to support the industry for at least the next five years. My hope is to have an expanded footprint in the space.

TAKEAWAYS

- Networking with other investors will make or break you in this investment class
- Accredited investors will have more opportunities, but it's possible to invest as a non-accredited investor in a 506(b)
- Diversify your timing, markets, and operators
- Consider joining investment clubs that have a focus on investing in syndication
- Consider starting your own investment LLC

6
LONG-TERM MORTGAGE NOTES

"If you learn how to solve the banks' problems, you are always going to have an opportunity as an investor."
—Bill McCafferty, Asset Manager for People's Mortgage Relief II, LLC

Be the bank. What a powerful concept for an investor to embrace. In Chapter 3, we looked at IBC policies—assets that are intended to give you control of your personal banking needs and, in essence, create your own bank. In this chapter, we'll look at how investing in residential mortgage notes is a natural complementary asset in your alternative investment portfolio because you actually get to use that personal bank in order to provide a mortgage to others.

It's fairly common for me to speak to investors who use their high-equity cash value policies to purchase individual mortgage notes. Remember, those policyholders look for ways to safely arbitrage the amount they would pay in interest on their cash value loan and the funds they would receive on their investment. Mortgage notes allow investors to accomplish this with a fair degree of certainty because of the reliability of the "hard asset" they are purchasing. That's not to say that the only way to invest in mortgage notes is through life insurance policies; both assets are merely tools that can be used together successfully.

What Is the Asset?

Put simply, a note is a contractual agreement to repay a loan between a borrower and a lender with set terms in place. When that contractual agreement is backed by real estate, then we refer to the note as a mortgage note.

A note can be originated by an institution (such as a bank) or by an individual. If an institution originates the mortgage, there is no guarantee that they will keep the mortgage on their own books. In fact, it's common practice for banks to take delinquent mortgages, pool them together, and sell them to private equity companies, hedge funds, and private investors. In turn, large pool buyers often resell individual mortgages to smaller investors.

Let's take a look at the other scenario, in which an individual originates the loan. For example, an investor who has a paid off a rental property may be looking to retire. But instead of selling their house for a one-time profit and being subject to the capital gains tax, the investor chooses to provide seller financing to the new owners. In this case, the investor would typically receive a down payment, followed by a stream of monthly payments for a set time period without having to deal with the stress of being a landlord. If the new borrower defaults, the original owner would foreclose on the property and take back the title while keeping the down payment as well as all of the payments that were made to date.

When the note is in good standing (less than 90 days past due), we call it a performing note. If the loan was delinquent but now is paid up to date, we call this a reperforming loan. If the loan goes over

90 days past due, it becomes a non-performing note. (Note: 90 days is a standard industry benchmark, but it can differ by contract.)

Residential mortgage notes like these are backed by the equity of the property, which provides security in case the borrower defaults on the mortgage. This is why we refer to mortgages as secured notes. There are also unsecured notes, but they tend to come with higher interest rates because they are inherently riskier; if a borrower defaults, there is no easy way to recover your investment as a lender.

It's important to note that these types of individual notes can be purchased by non-accredited investors, and in many ways, they provide many of the same benefits that smaller residential investments do—minus the legendary landlord stories. After all, when was the last time you heard a banker talk about getting a 2:00 a.m. toilet backup call?

When evaluating a note, it's important to factor in its position in relation to other existing debt on the property. The first debt placed on the property is referred to as the senior lien, and it takes priority over any other debt on the property. If there is not enough equity to pay the senior lien, the subsequent debt becomes insolvent. Because of the significance of the position of senior debt when it comes to repayment, a first position lien is considered a safer investment than a second-position lien or other junior lien, and it typically sells for lower yield. A huge misconception exists among borrowers that a second lien can't initiate a foreclosure on their property if the first position is in good standing. Some who face financial shortfalls even make a deliberate effort to only pay the first position and stop paying the second while ignoring multiple warnings of impending foreclosure proceedings. Only after learning that the foreclosure has started do they reach out to investors to try to work out terms to avoid losing their property.

Once an investor purchases a note, it can be serviced by a professional servicing company, which is akin to a property management company in real estate investing. They take care of the monthly management of payments, including ACH distributions; provide an online portal for the investor and the borrower; issue monthly statements and notices, including notices of default; and provide all necessary tax documents. (Note: You may think that taking care of all of this would cost a small fortune, but that's not the case. The cost is usually only around $15 per month with a small onboarding fee.)

A servicing company can also provide an investor with the ability to scale their note portfolio much faster than other alternative investments, as well as to diversify in multiple markets without having a traditional real estate team since most providers work nationwide and in accordance with local regulations. When diversifying in this way, an investor should focus on a few key characteristics, such as location, lien position, performing versus non-performing, and time to maturation. By tracking these variables in their portfolio, a note buyer can target specific notes in the future to round out their portfolio.

Many new investors in this space aren't aware that they can sell, partition, and even collateralize their notes because of the equity that's attached to them—or they can leave them intact and receive the full advantage of the borrower's payments over the complete amortization schedule, which may span 30 years like a traditional mortgage.

When it comes to selling a note, an investor has many options for exiting the investment. If the note is paid out early, then they receive a healthy premium since they would have to be paid back the full remaining unpaid principal all at once. For example, if there is a $100,000 unpaid balance, that note may be sold for $.80 on the dollar (or less if it's not performing). But if the note is paid off early, the full unpaid balance still needs to be paid off—not just the discounted price the secondary investor pays for it.

Partitioning a performing note allows an investor to recapture some of their invested capital by selling only a "partial,"[19] which is a portion of the income that is coming from the note. This can be done as a percentage of the existing yield or as a fixed stream of income for a set number of years. For example, a 15-year note could be split, with the original investor selling the first ten years of the note to another investor, while retaining just the last five years of income. This strategy can be a win-win for all: It provides immediate income for the secondary investor, and it allows the original investor to recoup the majority, if not all, of their initial investment, along with an income stream during the last five years (which actually *should* be the safest period of the loan because of the steady increase in equity over time). By selling partials in this way, investors can diversify when and how they will receive income over time. As you can see from this example, aside from factors

---

[19] "Partial purchase note offer," Amerinote Xchange (November 17, 2020), https://www.amerinotexchange.com/partial-purchase-note-offer/.

outside of the investor's control, notes provide incredible flexibility for investors who are looking for yield. Can you imagine getting that level of control with dividend-paying stocks?

Through the process of collateralization, the investor can take out a loan against their note's equity. Because the proceeds from the loan are tax-free, they can use them to continue investing in other non-Wall Street assets. If done correctly and conservatively, this process works effectively. While the note has to be in good standing before exercising this option, the equity provides reasonable assurances to the lender, which allows for favorable terms on the loan. Keep in mind that collateralization should not be confused with buying on margin, which involves borrowing money to invest. This is highly risky, and it is never recommended. Using collateral effectively can be systematized and repeated, whereas using margin is gambling—and eventually your luck will run out.

Before we move ahead, I want you to picture a scenario to envision how these processes work. In this scenario, there's an investor who we'll call Bob. Bob has a high-equity cash value life insurance policy with $300,000 of accumulated cash value. He uses that policy as collateral to loan himself money at a 5% interest rate to purchase a portfolio of performing notes in various markets with favorable demographics across the country. His monthly loan payments will be easily covered by the note portfolio that he has now placed in the hands of a servicing company, which manages all of the logistics of servicing the note, and he has not negatively affected his credit score by taking out this loan. After a year or so, Bob decides to partial his portfolio to recoup his $300,000 capital investment. He is still left with a portion of the income from the note portfolio after completely paying back the life insurance loan. Instead of partitioning the loan, Bob could have collateralized the note portfolio and used the funds to pay back the loan, which would have allowed Bob's investments to grow at a greater velocity. But in either case, the equity backing the collateral would have minimal correlation to Wall Street's volatility.

While rare, the exit plan for a mortgage note may involve foreclosing on a property if the borrower fails to keep up with their payments. If the note was purchased correctly with equity protecting the investment—and the borrower really wants nothing more to do with the property—then foreclosure may be the only viable option, but it should still provide a net positive benefit to the investor because they are assuming a property with built-in equity. Most note investors don't get into the business to foreclose, but it is a great back-up plan in this scenario.

As much as investors are painted as villains in certain circles, I often see note investors go out of their way to try to do what's best for borrowers when it comes to potential foreclosures. Just as the number one killer for small residential properties is vacancy, the same applies to note investing: Scale becomes an elusive dream if the note investor has to go around foreclosing on all of their borrowers. So generally speaking, foreclosures are a last resort. When a borrower falls behind in payments, they worry that their lender is going to take the property from them, and that sense of despair can spill over into the appearance of the property. But because note investors are not subject to bank rules, they can often change the terms of a loan to allow the borrower to catch up on missed payments. When that happens, their sense of dignity and pride in home ownership can be restored. In that way, the community as a whole can benefit when a note investor comes into the picture—unlike with stocks, where there are clear lines between select groups of winners and losers.

Of course, mortgage notes have some downsides. They include:

Tax planning requirements — Unless purchasing notes in a tax-deferred account like a self-directed IRA, a mortgage note does not provide the same favorable tax deductions as an investor in a single-family rental. As the "bank," you'll receive a 1099 form from the mortgage service provider, and the borrower will receive a 1098. This underscores why tax planning is essential with mortgage notes, just like any other real estate investment.

High demand/low supply — Because of recent historically low interest rates and often double-digit yields that are backed by a hard asset, mortgage notes have become a very popular asset class—and, as a result, the inventory of quality notes is dwindling. Most of the time, obtaining one involves competitively bidding against other investors.

No dramatic "end game" — At the end of the amortization schedule, the note investor is fully paid off, and there is no windfall of capital remaining. That's why it's important to mix in appreciation investments to balance high cash flow investments like mortgage notes.

Let's review:

- A note is a contractual agreement to repay a loan with fixed terms between a borrower and a lender.

- Notes can be originated by either an Institution like a bank or an individual.
- Notes can be secured or unsecured. Real estate investors focus on secured notes.
- Notes have different positions of debt repayment priority. First position (senior debt) has the highest priority, second position is next, and so on.
- Notes can be collateralized and partitioned.
- Notes can be sold on a secondary market after origination.
- Individual investors have multiple note exit points.
- Notes can be a complementary asset in an alternative investment portfolio, especially when paired with high-equity life insurance policies.

What Is the History of the Asset?

Mortgages trace their roots back to different ancient civilizations. While it's hard to pinpoint the exact origin, the modern-day American mortgage was shaped by the events of the Great Depression. Prior to the Great Depression, home mortgages were limited to 50% of a home's value and only had a term of between five to ten years. During the Great Depression, property prices collapsed, and many homeowners could not refinance their loan. Given the hefty down payment required at that time, many homeowners lost their entire net worth when their houses were foreclosed, with estimates as high as 1,000 foreclosed homes per day in 1933.[20]

---

[20] Kimberly Amadeo, "Mortgage history, types, and impact on the economy," The Balance (February 26, 2021), https://www.thebalance.com/what-is-a-mortgage-types-history-impact-3305946.

Franklin D. Roosevelt's New Deal proposed a few fundamental changes that would become the backbone of today's modern mortgages:

- First, FDR created the government-sponsored Home Owners' Loan Corporation, which purchased a million defaulted mortgages and then changed the terms to allow for a longer repayment period (this is exactly what non-performing note investors do).
- Second, the Federal Housing Administration was created to provide mortgage insurance, allowing for smaller down payments.
- Next, the Federal National Mortgage Association (commonly known as Fannie Mae) created a market for loans if banks needed to get them off of their balance sheets.
- The Federal Deposit Insurance Corporation followed suit, giving homeowners reassurance that their money wouldn't disappear if their bank went out of business.
- Last, the Glass-Steagall Act put restrictions on how banks could invest their deposited funds (although this was later largely repealed).

The end result was an infinitely more affordable and stable asset that still plays a prominent role for all note investors.

What Are the Current Regulations on Buying and Selling the Asset?

Mortgage notes are subject to both federal and state regulations. As an investor, you need to work with licensed professionals, including attorneys, title companies, and servicing companies. Many times, if you find one professional that you like, they can make referrals that will build out the team needed to legally buy and manage a note portfolio. When possible, make sure that the professionals you choose are audited, which is common practice in the mortgage service industry. By working with providers that have a national presence, you can mitigate a lot of the potential compliance risks, but the responsibility of making sure you are federally and state compliant is on you. One great source of information is experienced note investors in your state.

What Is the Market for the Asset?
Notes can usually be purchased from one of four sources:

Online networking — There are different online groups that can connect brokers to investors, but it doesn't happen overnight. Some brokers have strong relationships with note buyers, sellers, and institutions that new investors can tap into. Brokers can also help you remain compliant during the transaction. Like any other type of brokerage business, some brokers are only concerned with collecting their fees, and others put an emphasis on building relationships. While both types of brokers can provide you with access to deals, you can guess which type will help you grow as an investor.

Loan exchanges — While larger institutions use their own trade desks to sell their notes, smaller community banks contract out the service to loan exchanges, which then provide an online portal where investors bid on notes.

Servicing companies — Since they are actively managing notes, it's a natural fit for some servicing companies to provide a means of buying and selling them, as well.

Note funds — If you're an accredited investor, you can invest in a fund that operates exclusively in notes. The returns are usually lower with this approach, but you receive instant diversification within a large pool of notes that is run by professionals. A great resource for fund recommendations is BiggerPockets, as some prominent experts in this space are very active in this community. I started in notes using this method, and that investment helped me establish credibility when I began talking to other investors. The note fund's monthly newsletter also regularly taught me something new about the industry.

The Bad Apples: Has Anybody Committed Fraud in This Asset Class?

Fraud is much more prevalent in the promissory note space, where there is less equity backing the investment. But because the onus on finding deals in mortgage notes is on the investor (and, in fact, it should be a red flag if you're new and being approached with inventory available for purchase), there is a chance of buying a bad note or overpaying for a good note. However, this is less about fraud and more about learning how to conduct proper due diligence.

The multiple professionals involved in the process may mitigate any attempts at outright fraud, and knowing how to analyze a deal properly will help you avoid losing money on bad investments. When in doubt, network, network, network!

What Are the Lessons to Be Learned?

From a macro perspective, one of my favorite characteristics of mortgage notes is that they perform well in both bull and bear markets, as long as investors remain diversified and space out the timing of their investments.

In a bull market, fewer people default on their loans. People have more money to pay their mortgage, and they usually feel richer because the prices for their investments are rising. This leads to increasing property values and a shorter supply of both homes and notes. Remember: Notes are backed by equity, so as property values increase, the original note actually becomes a safer investment. This allows the investors to exit deals (by refinancing or selling) at a faster rate (which bodes well for IRR% and the time value of money). The same note can also be resold quicker to take advantage of the equity spread that just occurred.

In a bear market, people have a tougher time paying their mortgage. This leads to more delinquencies which, in turn, floods the market with new inventory that can be picked up for a considerable discount.

If you're going to invest in notes, you need to be able to analyze them in the same way you would analyze a rental property. Just because there are fewer tenant headaches doesn't mean the numbers are any less important in this asset class.

The Pros and Cons of Investing in Long-Term Mortgage Notes

PROS

- A note represents a hard asset backed by the equity of the property
- Investor enjoys all of the amortization benefits of a bank
- Potential large payday if the loan is closed prior to end of term since remaining balance needs to be paid off, and notes are usually purchased at a discount
- Great for passive cash flow
- No fixing toilets or leaking roofs
- Mortgage can be serviced by a professional servicing company for a very reasonable fee
- Easy to diversify between various geographic locations, school districts, lien positions, etc.
- Third-party market exists where you can collateralize the notes, sell a piece of the note, or sell the entire note
- Socially conscious investing (if done right)
- Non-accredited investors can purchase individual notes

CONS

- Unfavorable tax treatment (some investors prefer to buy these only in tax-advantaged retirement plans)
- Foreclosure a possibility in case of default
- High demand during low-yield environments
- Many state and federal regulations
- No principal left after the owner pays off the note

ASK THE EXPERTS: Q&A With David Putz

Disclaimer: This Q&A is provided for informational purposes only. You should seek your own advice from professional advisors, including lawyers, financial advisors, and accountants, regarding the legal, tax, and financial implications of any investment you contemplate.

David Putz has been an active real estate investor since 2010. He has worked with rentals, fix & flips, and a large private equity fund, where he completed due diligence on property valuations. As managing member of JKP Holdings LLC, David evaluates and manages deals and raises funds for the purchase of mortgage notes nationwide.

When did you start investing?

In 2005, I bought my first rental property after a series of discussions with a couple of my friends. We got into it thinking that it was a great time to take action for where the market was in its cycle, and we were excited to start learning how to become landlords. We were buying in our local area mainly for appreciation, renting out the units, and growing from there. The idea of having a cash-flowing asset in combination with the ability to appreciate in the long run, was the angle I was going for. To get started, I lived in the house that I went on to rent out.

How were you introduced to mortgage notes?

In 2008, after a few years of owning rental properties, my childhood friend introduced me to notes. He was working for a note company at that time. While sitting around the table talking, he would tell me what he was doing, and our conversations got me interested in learning more about the space. I just started diving into the fundamentals, along with the nuances that came along with investing in notes. I didn't invest at that time, but I saw what I needed to see: This was a completely different model than my rental properties.

Two years later, I was helping a friend of mine, who was just getting started in note investing. He wanted help evaluating notes and the assets behind them. We evaluated close to 3,000 assets in a couple of days. I gave him an idea of what I thought the value was, what the market was, what would it look like from a visual point of view, etc. After that exercise, I realized that in the note space, I wouldn't have to deal with the same issues I was having with my rentals, I wouldn't have to deal with in the note space. I realized I couldn't do rentals anymore, and I bought my first note in 2012.

What is the biggest negative you discovered?

I would say the negative in this asset class is the unknowns. Legally, you need to know what you can and can't do. The insurance side of it. The force placement side of it. I would say that's the hardest part, and it just comes with experience and asking other people around you.

Also, most notes weren't in my backyard, so I didn't know the areas as well as my local rental market. Also, how to fund the deals was the other big negative. You need actual cash and capital to do this; you can't go get a loan for a property like you can for rentals. Thankfully, I had a friend who was going through the process, and

I could lean on him for advice and leverage his 30,000 notes of experience. It was a great way to fast track the process and get through the trials and tribulations that came up.

I created systems to work with agents to learn about local markets and how to assess the true value of properties, which gave me confidence to pursue deals nationwide. That was a big departure from my rental days. I then addressed capital concerns. In the first couple of deals, I used my own money. Then I started doing joint ventures, and it took a while to get over that fear of bringing other people's money to the deal. I eventually started my own private equity firm with my partner.

What is your most memorable experience in this asset class?

One specific experience I remember is that we bought a note that was part of a larger pool. Initially, we had a slam dunk on our hands. We got ahold of the borrower, and they were eager to sign over the property since they knew nothing about it. That's when the deal fell apart. Shortly after, we found a second position loan on the property. We reached out to the owner of the second position loan to find out they didn't know anything about the lien being there. We then realized that the property condition was worse than we thought and was only worth like $4,000–$5,000. The ARV (After Repair Value) was only $50k. A couple weeks later, the owner of the second lien finally found the lien and valued it at $20k. We had to write off almost the entire value of the note.

The other most notable negative experience was an asset that we bought knowing that the property was damaged. We knew the date and the time the damage occurred, and I was ecstatic about being able to file for the insurance to get the whole payout. I came to find out that the type of policy that the force placed insurance was under prohibited the insurance payout. I spoke to the insurance company, which was my insurance company. They said because of the way the policy was written, there was no way to go back and file claim on it because the seller had to file prior to closing the deal. That oversight on my end turned into a very memorable $30k loss. It's safe to say we never made the same mistake again.

What is a common misconception about mortgage notes?

It's how to calculate the deal. New investors have adopted a Nike mentality of "Just do it" and jump in headfirst. But you need to understand some fundamentals and make sure you're jumping in the right kind of asset, preferably a performing note to lower your risk.

Joint venturing is big in this space, but you shouldn't get into that when you're brand new because it's very easy for an SEC violation to occur. If you're joint venturing strictly for capital, and your partner brings the capital and remains passive in the deal, but you're doing everything else, you might think that this is a win-win. But, in reality, you unknowingly created a security, and the consequences of that can be pretty severe regardless of your intentions.

What is the most important thing an investor should know when considering a mortgage note?

Is the note already performing? I like to compare notes to rentals because it's probably the easiest comparison. When you buy a *property, you can fix it up, and then flip it. You can do that with notes, too. You can buy a non-performing loan, rehab the loan, and as it begins to perform, you can then sell it. Similarly, you can also buy a property, fix it up, and rent it. Same with a note: You can buy a note, fix it up, and hold it performing. It's the same mindset, right? You have your servicer, who is actually your property manager. Same concept.*

Knowing what state the note is in is a huge thing. If it's in New Jersey versus Texas, that matters. Certain states are faster to foreclose than other states. The other thing an investor should pay attention to is whether a debt license is required by that state. So if you're buying in Kansas or Kentucky, you need a license to collect debt. Without going out to get your own license, your servicer can be the only means of your debt collection. I wouldn't even entertain investing in notes as a new investor if I didn't plan on using a servicing company. The Fair Debt Collection Practices Act, which notes are subject to, is very specific about what can and can't be done. That's why you need a good servicing company that works well within the rules.

What is your professional background, and how did it affect your investing career?

Zero. My professional background is non-real estate. My day job is clinical work for the state. I have a natural inclination towards technology and spreadsheets, and that has helped me with notes, but nothing transferrable from my professional background.

What information sources have been the most influential for you?

Networking with other investors in person and on different social media channels, like Facebook, LinkedIn, and the BiggerPockets community. I think it's the number one thing that will predict your investing longevity: These networking events and conferences where you can meet people who have such diverse backgrounds, and we can barter our systems for mutual profit.

There are also a ton of different books I've read over the years from Rich Dad Poor Dad *to just general mentality books and making sure you're striving to become a better version of you.*

Who that you personally know do you most respect in business, and why?

Jack Krupey, a childhood friend who did incredibly well in this space. We've been friends for 35 years now. His mind is amazing; he's a different level than most investors I know. I admire him, but I can't correlate with him. I'm always trying to pick his brain about everything he's doing and investing in. He gets ahead by just pushing through obstacles. Even though he's extremely successful, he'd rather not talk about business. He's a very big networker who can fill a conference in a heartbeat. But it's when you lock him down for an hour, and he has to get something done that he can outperform anyone. He can compete with attorneys and argue points, and he has an amazing memory. He just grasps things faster than you do, and he doesn't understand why you don't.

I'm also fond of people who are good at things I'm not good at, such as marketing. I'm a terrible marketer, but I respect those who are great at it or find the way to doing it. It is something that doesn't come easy to me, and I don't find the value in it sometimes.

You are at a holiday party and asked what you do for a living. What do you say?

I raise private money and invest in real estate nationwide. That's a cliché thing to say, but anything more leads to lots of questions and confusion. It also depends on the person, right? If the person understands what that means, I know I can go deeper into real estate.

I'm always looking to gain and learn something by a conversation; that's just how I'm built. I always feel like the guy sitting next to me at the bar can tell me so many things I just don't know about.

What is the best piece of investing advice that you've ever received?

Be who you are. We all have value, and we should work on that value, whatever it is. Also, don't try to reach up to the highest level when you get started. Just find someone one step above you and work with them. You don't have to be talking to a guy with $33 billion worth of deals. You're not there. Talk to the person with three deals that can directly relate to what you are doing.

My last piece of advice is to network with different people. Some people get linked into one guru/expert—and they lock on to them—where I may see things differently than another person even if they're in my niche. No one's right; no one's wrong. But just collectively listen to what we're saying and make your own decision.

You'll find that some deals have killer returns, but the returns come second to this experience of networking with the other investors in the space. You become really good friends. It's a very close community that you really can lean on, unlike other real estate classes. You're cooperating to a point, and you're competing to a point—but you're not fully doing either one of them.

What's your greatest alternative investment failure, and what would you do differently?

We invested in two movies, and they did nothing. It's been four or five years now. And the money is pretty much gone, and it's not looking good. The person we invested with was from the note space and raised a lot of money from the note community. I bought my first few deals from him, and we had a great relationship. When the deal started to go bad, he basically started avoiding phone calls, ignoring emails, and fell off the Earth. I don't think he deliberately set out to do anything wrong. I think he just didn't know how to get out of it because it was a space he wasn't sure of. One of the movies was going to be in the movie theater, and COVID hit, and that was definitely bad luck. In the end, we lost money, and the fallout was us losing a really good friend in the deal.

I hate to say I wouldn't do the deal again, but I should have listened to my gut. Unfortunately, there were three of us in my immediate circle that invested, and we usually lean on each other for advice. If one of us would have backed out, we probably all would have, but we all got suckered in. We're now more hesitant about doing deals that we don't have much information about. I can do a note deal knowing what my exit options are, but with the movies, I had no idea how to exit if the movie wasn't successful. I ended up finding out the answer: you don't.

In five years, do you still see yourself investing in this niche?

I would like to see where the space is. When I started in 2012, there was tons of inventory, where that's not the case today. Maybe with COVID, there will be an influx of inventory. Hopefully, I am smart enough to realize when investing in notes isn't working anymore and move on to do something different. I want to invest in assets that are on sale, and certain notes are still on sale, but it's not the way it used to be. I'd be an irresponsible investor to stay with something simply because I like it, right? There's always that risk of staying in something a little too long or not long enough.

ASK THE EXPERTS: Q&A With Bill McCafferty

Disclaimer: This Q&A is provided for informational purposes only. You should seek your own advice from professional advisors, including lawyers, financial advisors, and accountants, regarding the legal, tax, and financial implications of any investment you contemplate.

Bill McCafferty is a full-time asset manager for People's Mortgage Relief II, LLC. He has over 15 years of experience in all aspects of residential real estate and has managed well over 1,000 reperforming and non-performing second mortgages. He really enjoys assisting other note investors in the business, in whatever way possible.

When did you start investing?

My first of investment of any kind was early on with traditional savings. A lot of people overlook the fact that just a savings account is the real first step to becoming an investor. Later on, when I got my first job at the age of 21, I took advantage of my employer's 401(k). As much as I did not know the full details of what a 401(k) was, what they were actually doing, or what mutual funds were, I did understand the fact that I could put money in a retirement account, my company would match me, and the company was going to then go invest that money, and it was going to be for me later on in life. I think that's definitely a start that a lot of people overlook. In 2006, I bought my first rental property. That's when it all started clicking.

How were you introduced to your specific niche?

My first job out of college, I was working at a school taking care of the athletic fields and running a shop for kids. I was kind of moving through life and settling for average. Sometime in my late 20s, it kind of smacked me in the face that if I was going to continue to bring home the paycheck that I was bringing home, I was selling myself short. I just hit a wall. I did a lot of soul searching and started envisioning the life that I really wanted to get to. One night, I was sitting on the couch watching TV, and I saw an infomercial on buying real estate with no money down. I thought this is probably *a scam, and it's probably not as easy as the commercial is making it out to be, but there's got to be something to this.*

I've always been a believer that if you want to do something or learn something, just go find people that are doing it. So in 2005, I started going to investment groups and local real estate groups, and seeing what other people were doing. After about 24 months, it really all started clicking. There were some investors that were well respected in these groups that were buying delinquent residential second mortgages. By networking with them, I was able to block out a lot of nonsense. Even with their help, it was a lot of trial and error early on. At first, I invested in rentals. Some of them worked out, but some did not.

From 2007–2009, I invested in a note fund with the same investors from my group. That allowed me to get a better look at what they were doing. A year later, I bought a reperforming loan and began to see the payments come in. In 2009, I bought my first non-performing second position loan. Right away, I had some pretty cool success with it. I was able to actually get some money wired to me the day before a foreclosure sale. I was out with my family that day when I got a notification that the money was sent. That moment was the culmination of all my investing experiences, relationships, soul searching, and trying to figure out a better way.

At that point, I was still very much in the rat race working 40–50 hours a week making money for someone else. I was not seeing my family as much as I would like. At that time, I had young kids, and I was worried about whether I was going to be able to go watch their sporting events in high school, or if I'd be buried at a company working long hours. My wife was doing the same thing, 40–50 hours a week. We were both coming home stressed out, not wanting to put the time and energy into our family. I needed something completely different. That investment was proof that there was a better option out there. It was my version of the American Dream.

I say it all the time: Was I in the right place at the right time, or did I take massive action? It's definitely a combination of both. I do know that I was in a great place at the right time, but I got myself there. It's funny how it works, but I'm a big advocate of things happen for a reason.

What is the biggest negative you discovered?

Everyone's got an opinion, but take financial advice with a grain of salt if that person doesn't own any assets or have any money. You might have a lot of good people around you that say they don't want to see you fail and that they love you. But the truth is there's a lot of jealousy out there—a lot of the "if I can't do it, he's not going to be able to do it" mentality. You have to learn how to position yourself around successful people and not allow that negativity to occupy your brain and your space, or it will absolutely destroy you. Even now, I talk to people all the time that tell me they've heard this business is done, and there's nothing left out there. But I keep doing my thing and positioning myself to move forward in this space.

What is your most memorable experience in this asset class?

It allowed my wife to retire before the age of 40 to be at home with my kids and to take care of all the things around me. This allowed me to concentrate on the business and have the family life I dreamed of. I was attending a college tour yesterday with my son, and one of the things that came up with the football coach was that my son played 12 years of football, and I only missed one game because I was in the hospital. That stuff is important to me. I'm a huge advocate that financial freedom is not about the money; it's about the time. The fact is that money buys you time. This asset class has allowed me to take control of my financial dashboard and my life. It has allowed me to live my American dream.

What is a common misconception about mortgage notes?

A big misconception is that it's easy. In real estate and in business, in general, a lot of people just want to throw money at a problem and think that will always solve it and the underlying issues. Well, it's not always about the money. It's about the systems. It's about the organization. It's about the discipline. It's about putting in your 10,000 hours.

What is the most important thing an investor should know when considering a mortgage note?

Regulations and compliance are the biggest concerns in the note space right now. It was the Wild West back when I started; you could do anything, anywhere. Now it's all regulated. You need to pay attention and be careful.

What is your professional background, and how did it affect your investing career?

I graduated with a Sociology/Criminal Justice degree. Sociology is the study of human beings, and at the end of the day, every business has human beings. You need to learn how to deal with them in a fair manner. The art of the deal in the delinquent mortgage space is learning how to deal with attorneys, disgruntled homeowners, and investors—and not allow the emotions to crush you.

One thing that I learned from my first job at the school (that I mentioned earlier) was how to deal with every type of person at every age group, from every culture, every race, and everybody in between—people that were handed silver spoons, and people that weren't. Most importantly, I learned how to listen to people and respect what they have to say. During 15 years of taking care of the school's athletic facilities, I learned what it takes to get stuff done and how to stay organized.

Your name is everything in business. I've been in this space close to 15 years, and I take a lot of pride in my name. I think that with anybody you talk to, you're not going to hear anything bad about me. I have homeowners who I helped resolve their problems with delinquent mortgages, and now I'm friends with them on social media, and they still text or call me to this day. It's those little things. When I resolve issues with homeowners, even if it's a client's file and not my own note, I always let them know they can call me even if it's a few years down the line.

What information sources have been the most influential for you?

My education mainly comes from getting around the correct people and working hard to master my craft. My network has been huge for me, including my mentors at Partners for Payment Relief (PPR): Dave Van Horn, John Sweeney, and Bob Paulus. I listened to a lot of their podcasts early on. Also, the book Paper Profits: How to Buy and Profit From Notes: A Beginner's Guide *by my friend Josh Andrews.*

Who that you personally know do you most respect in business, and why?

This business has led to many lifelong friendships. I previously mentioned the partners at PPR, but besides them, there's Fred Moskowitz, a good buddy who invests in the mortgage space. We enjoy a lot of the same things in life, like prioritizing family. Every year, we connect to do our goals together. It's something I look forward to very much.

There's also Steve Lloyd, an investor who introduced me to notes. With some mentors, just being able to see what they're doing and how they handle and carry themselves is enough.

You are at a holiday party and asked what you do for a living. What do you say?

I build portfolios of institutional residential reperforming and non-performing second mortgage notes for myself and for my clients, which in return, builds cash flow and wealth. Sometimes that response is enough, and we move on. Other times, it starts great conversations.

What is the best piece of investing advice that you've ever received?

Especially early on, I always had a resource to talk to and to get advice from. There's really only two ways to success, and that's through mentors and mistakes. As long as you learn from your mistakes, even if you make them a few times, you're going to just keep getting better and better. It's the same thing with mentors, whether a paid mentor or somebody that you create value for who can also help you out.

I have a very good friend who I grew up with named Phil, who's in the investment world. He's registered with the SEC and has about $500 million of assets under management. He's a very smart guy who does very well, a natural hustler. Everybody says this, but he's the first one who drilled this statement into my head: I always want to be the dumbest guy in the room. He probably has about 40 employees, and he'll be the first one to tell you that everyone who works for him is smarter than him.

What's your greatest alternative investment failure, and what would you do differently?

I wish I came into the real estate world a little slower. A lot of investors advise buying one rental per year. If I would have followed that advice, I would have a much larger rental portfolio today. When I first started, I bought 20 properties in one year and leveraged myself to the brink before the market crashed. Things didn't work out well. As much as I love the note business, I now don't own enough brick and mortar because of how fast I went when I started. So I wish I could tell my younger self to slow down.

In five years, do you still see yourself investing in this niche?

Absolutely. I'm not going anywhere. The space is not going anywhere. There are so many segments in the industry:

institutional, first position, second position, partial loans, or investments through funds. The delinquent note space is a full-time job that requires a heavy time commitment, so eventually the goal is to have enough notes in my own name where I can dial it down a little bit. Right now, I'm investing in the generation of note investors that's following us. I believe that it will pay dividends when I decide to become more passive.

TAKEAWAYS

- Complementary asset to high-equity life insurance policies
- Great alternative to single-family home rentals
- Unique win-win situation in any market cycle
- Not tax friendly, but an investor can use a self-directed IRA or a similar retirement vehicle to offset taxes
- Backed by the equity of a hard asset
- A service provider acts as a property manager for the note

7
MOBILE HOME PARKS

"There is more to the manufactured housing community asset class than what is taught in podcasts and bootcamps; it is not 'hands off.' It is more helpful to think of it as a business rather than simply a class of rental properties."
—Jared Surnamer, President of Valley Community Management

Close your eyes and think about the following three words: mobile home park. What comes to mind? Do you imagine a family-friendly community or a daunting trailer park? Most likely, your first vision isn't a positive one, and you're not alone. Because mobile home parks are viewed so unfavorably by the majority of counties in this country, there have been very few built during the last two decades. Despite their vexing negative reputation, the truth is that most parks are safe, welcoming, and affordable living environments. Newer homes often include higher end features like open-concept kitchens with granite countertops and stainless steel appliances, and certain parks even offer Class A amenities, like in-grounds pools, picnic areas, dog parks, and more at a fraction of the price of similar living arrangements. Due to a lack of other comparable and affordable options, residents rarely move out of nice parks; and since most of them own their homes, the high cost of moving incentivizes them to stay put for years or even decades.

The parks that exist today were developed in the 1970s and 80s and have aged accordingly. What were once well-run businesses in their prime have deteriorated into a mere shell of their former condition. The operators, often mom-and-pop business owners, often have retired, and their next of kin want nothing to do with the family business. The result is many neglected parks that have begun rapidly changing hands in the current environment. What was once a dirty phrase in the investment world, mobile home parks have become as desirable as any other asset class in this book.

I invested in my first mobile home park in 2019. It was a 53-lot community located in Topeka, Kansas. Through networking, I met a reputable mobile home property operating team that specialized in heavy value-add deals. In general, these types of deals tend to have poor cash flow in the earlier phases of the business plan, but because there is significant upside when the value-add is completed, can become very lucrative later.

The park we purchased was half vacant, and we got a great deal with owner financing in place. Owner financing is much more of a norm in the mobile home park space than in other commercial real estate niches. That's because in many cases, like this one, the low vacancy rates of a run-down park would disqualify it for any other type of financing. With this project, I was able to participate in the operations calls and have access to the property management software, which allowed me to see in real time what was going on in the park. The experience was a real eye opener. During the first year and a half of ownership, we dealt with a tenant uprising that culminated in city officials being summoned and a tenant purposely flushing garbage down the toilet (a really *shitty* situation, if you'll pardon the expression). In turn, this caused a sewer backup to half of the park's residents and a hefty excavation expense, numerous evictions, and multiple police calls—essentially, every stereotypical negative outcome you might associate with investing in mobile home parks.

But what came next was an amazing turnaround in the park: We rebranded it with a beautiful entryway, added floodlights and fences around the perimeter to increase safety, removed a few tenants that were clearly involved in drug trafficking, raised our tenant eligibility criteria, and improved the exteriors on multiple homes. In the near future, our investment in the park should become profitable. Next, my investment fund, SIH Capital Group, plans on creating an annual scholarship for our residents at the park. In all, these initiatives will have a positive impact on a total of 53 families. Never before have I been able to use an investment to effect such significant social change. As you can see, these types of opportunities are not without their challenges, but they can be life-changing when you can partner with the right operators who share an innovative vision.

What Is the Asset?
A mobile home park is piece of land that has been sectioned into lots with utility hookups that allow for the establishment of a community of manufactured homes.

Mobile home parks have three distinct business models:

Park-owned homes — In this scenario, the park operator owns each of the mobile homes and is therefore responsible for all maintenance and repairs inside the park and homes. Most owners shy away from this model because even though the rent they charge is higher, it is partially offset by the higher operating expenses. However, from a strict revenue perspective, this gives investors the most bang for their investment buck.

Tenant-owned homes — This is considered a more attractive model in today's investing environment. In fact, out of all of the mobile home communities that currently exist in the United States, roughly 71.1% of the homes are tenant-owned.[21] In this scenario, the homes are owned by the tenants, and the owner rents out the land and utility hookups. The tenant pays for the lot rent and any utility expenses that are in their name, and they are responsible for all maintenance and upkeep issues. Usually, the need for property management is minimal, and the economics of the model don't support it anyway. In some cases, lot rents are only $200–$300 per month, so a 10% management fee only equates to about $20–$30 per month. It's not easy to attract quality property management at those rates.

Hybrid model — This is a combination of park-owned and tenant-owned homes. Often, the operator's goal is to convert to a fully tenant-owned model by selling the homes to their tenants. In some cases, an older home may even be given away at no cost if the new owner agrees to make repairs and pay the lot rents. This is one reason why investors don't often place

---

[21] Sydney Bennett, "Are manufactured homes a solution to the housing affordability crisis?", Apartment List (June 15, 2018), https://www.apartmentlist.com/research/mobile-homes-affordability-crisis.

extensive weight on the sale of homes when considering an investment.

What Is the History of the Asset?

Mobile home parks trace their roots to the 16th century when gypsies traveled in mobile homes carried by horses.[22] In the United States, mobile homes appeared on the scene late in the 19th century on the shores of North Carolina. Once again, poor horses were tasked with moving the homes. Fifty years later, travel trailers were introduced, which were similar to modern-day campers attached to a truck via a hitch. Due to their limited production and high prices, they were considered a luxury accessory for the rich used primarily for camping trips. The big critical mass moment happened after World War II, when veterans were coming home ready to start a new life, and housing was in short supply. Within three years of the end of the war, the length of the standard mobile home increased to 30 feet, and for the first time, the homes included bathrooms. This led to the introduction of the double-wide mobile home.

In 1974, due to concerns about the safety of mobile homes, Congress passed the National Manufactured Housing Construction and Safety Act, which set federal standards for building guidelines and established the new term of "manufactured homes." Ironically, from that point on, there has been very little development in

---

[22] Mary Bellis, "The history of mobile homes," ThoughtCo (March 5, 2019), https://www.thoughtco.com/history-of-mobile-homes-4076982.

manufacturing home communities with a widespread ban on new communities.

What Are the Current Regulations on Buying and Selling the Asset?
While there are no real restrictions on purchasing a mobile home park, investing in a syndication or fund typically requires accredited status.

In addition, at this point, most existing parks are grandfathered in, giving them a solid competitive advantage when compared to other asset classes—especially self-storage. However, there are "sunset provisions" that can be enacted by certain municipalities that remove a park's grandfathered protection and deem it unlivable. Once this happens, it is very difficult to reverse, so you'll want to ensure that you do due diligence prior to investing in any deal. If you're looking to purchase a park on your own, you will want to make sure the park is in good standing with the town in which it's located.

The second major regulatory concern is any potential negative environmental impact from the existing utility structure underneath a park. If you are dealing with city utilities, you are most likely in the clear. However, private utilities can get expensive and downright nasty to deal with. Make sure the operators you're investing in have a clear plan when it comes to utilities. Any environmental issues are usually uncovered during what's called a Phase 1 report. If a Phase 2 report is needed, which is the major conclusion of a Phase 1 report, then you should walk away as a new investor.

A note about foreclosure in this asset class: If a tenant stops paying rent, the process of retaking the property is surprisingly simple. In most states, mobile homes are considered personal property and may only require a visit to the DMV for the park operator to assume the title. In some cases, the tenant who owns the house will just abandon or sign over the home to the park because the overdue lot rent paired with the expense of moving the home are more costly than just leaving. This process can range from a few weeks to a few months, depending on the county in which the park is located. If the home is dilapidated beyond repair, it can be replaced by a new home relatively inexpensively or through financing programs available directly to the new tenant. Keep in mind that if an operator is dealing with multiple infills—the process of populating a lot with new mobile homes—they may be required to become a licensed dealer, depending on the requirements in their specific state.

What Is the Market for the Asset?

There is a huge shortage of affordable housing in this country, making the market surprisingly brisk for mobile homes, which have an average sale price of only $84,600.[23] Today, there are over 6.7 million existing occupied manufactured homes in the United States, and nearly 40% of new manufactured homes are placed in land-leased communities[24] with an average length of tenancy that is measured in decades. With only a handful of new parks having

[23] Andrew Kern, "Why manufactured housing is the new affordable housing," *Commercial Property Executive* (October 2020), https://www.cpexecutive.com/post/why-manufactured-housing-is-the-new-affordable-housing/.

[24] Ibid.

been built after the 1970s due to municipalities not willing to approve them in their jurisdictions, the end result is a pent-up demand for existing parks and empty lots in well-placed markets. Nearly half of all manufactured home communities are located in rural areas away from the urban core; however, there is a growing interest in suburban areas.

The Bad Apples: Has Anybody Committed Fraud in This Asset Class?

There isn't as much fraud in this space as there is a misconception about what the asset class really stands for. As an investor, I deal with operators who continually attempt to improve the quality of life for their tenants, as well as to change the negative connotations surrounding the industry, as a whole. These operators are mindful that 22 million people in the United States live in manufactured homes with an average median household income under $30,000.[25] These facts mean something to my operators, and investing in this space allows them to help their residents find a place that they can proudly call home.

It's worth noting that bad public relations stemming from rent increases is a real concern for operators in this space. It is often perceived as operators taking advantage of low-income residents, even when the increases are minor and appropriate for the market. For this reason, most operators exercise an abundance of caution and space out rent increases to multiple years.

---

[25] Ibid.

What Are the Lessons to Be Learned?

As an investor, it's vital to ensure that your operator is comparing apples to apples when considering the purchase of a new mobile home park. They cannot accurately compare the net operating income of a park-owned model to a tenant-owned model. If they do, they won't be able to convert the park-owned homes in the future without everyone missing their projected numbers. Some sellers try to glorify the numbers associated with park-owned homes, but the numbers need to be adjusted based on the business model. If your plan is to convert to an all tenant-owned model, what will the NOI be strictly based on lot rents, without factoring in any other additional revenue (including the sale of the homes during the conversion from a park-owned to tenant-owned model)? The offer price should be based on this total sum.

PRO TIP: *When starting out, anticipate that one-third of the deals that are supposed to generate cash flow very well will become larger projects than expected and instead cash flow poorly. This means that if you try to create a portfolio by mixing together cash flow projects with value-add projects, you should skew the projects toward the former; in the long run, you will achieve balance. If you try to balance your portfolio evenly from Day 1, your cash flow will fall short of what you expect. Over time, your ratio will improve with more selective selection of deals and operators.*

The Pros and Cons of Investing in Mobile Home Parks
PROS
- A better opportunity to purchase "off market" deals
- Potentially more favorable seller financing terms
- Most affordable option for home ownership

- Easier foreclosure process, as some states view the homes as personal property
- Great tenant retention rates
- Great value-add opportunities with aging communities

CONS

- Bad PR for rent raises
- Not viewed favorably by surrounding communities
- Dealer's license needed in some cases to infill lots
- Complicated utility systems when not connected to public utilities
- Lack of professional property management options

ASK THE EXPERTS: Q&A With Richard Sherman

Disclaimer: This Q&A is provided for informational purposes only. You should seek your own advice from professional advisors, including lawyers, financial advisors, and accountants, regarding the legal, tax, and financial implications of any investment you contemplate.

Richard Sherman is an expert in large-scale contract negotiations with complex and long-term sales processes. He has over 15 years of experience in enterprise contract negotiation and sales with clients including Nike, Microsoft, Amazon, Expedia, Honeywell, HTC, Weyerhaeuser, Russel Investments, and Starbucks. Richard and his wife own and self-manage approximately 100 apartments and single-family homes just south of Portland, Oregon, and approximately 600 mobile home pads across 11 mobile home parks.

When did you start investing?

We bought our first 4-plex property in Oregon in late 2007, just in time to get our teeth kicked in. We bought two of them right at the top of the market, and we just sold them last year . . . wonderful return [laughing]. More than doubled plus all the rents we collected for the 11 years we had them. That's the funny thing about real estate: Just wait long enough, and your most boneheaded decisions will look brilliant. We bought our first mobile home park in 2016.

How were you introduced to mobile home parks?

After reading about them and hearing some REITs that were getting into them big time, I thought I bet there is a niche for the ones that are too small or don't fit what the REITs want for other reasons (small towns—which I love—vacancy, etc.)

What is the biggest negative you discovered?

The amount of work and specialized knowledge needed to deal with the trailers themselves and the park infrastructure. I thought that specialized knowledge can become an unfair advantage for us if we get really good at it. I like assets with barriers to entry.

What is your most memorable experience in this asset class?

Finding out an on-site manager we had was stealing supplies and selling them, including appliances. Huge problem. You really have *to manage your managers. Runner up: Someone who we had to kick out threw about 30 dirty diapers on the floor of the trailer on the way out!*

What is a common misconception about mobile home parks?

They have certainly become hot, so I think much of the stigma is gone now, or I would have said the "trailer park stigma." I think the biggest misconception is that it is less work than apartments. No way! I think they can be when you get them full of newer tenant-owned trailers, but the real money is in the heavy lift to get them from high vacancy to full, and from park-owned homes to tenant-owned homes. Parks are just as management intensive as apartments, maybe slightly more due to pet and parking issues.

What is the most important thing an investor should know when considering a mobile home park?

Invest with someone who has experience in this space. Mobile home parks take a very different skill set than other residential investments. It requires much more specialized knowledge and problem-solving to deal with vacancies and the nuances of the trailers, in general (buying, remodeling, maintaining, moving, demoing, etc.), which is very different than any other residential asset class. There are also lots of pitfalls (zoning, public versus private utilities, etc.).

What is your professional background, and how did it affect your investing career?

Technology and technology sales. As our income went up, we just kept plowing it into real estate, and I am very happy that we did.

What information sources have been the most influential for you?

I enjoy BiggerPockets. I think much of the content is not aimed at me, but I enjoy it anyway. I like how scrappy and inventive people are. I also like MacroVoices, a broader investment podcast, though it can be pretty dry and nerdy.

I think that Mobile Home University has a lot of value operationally for a new owner. The forums specifically are of great value, as there are lots of things you never imagined would happen or questions you never thought to ask, and you can generally find some insight there (not always the right answer, but at least some ideas on how people have dealt with it in the past).

Who that you personally know do you most respect in business, and why?

There are a couple that can be on this list. I am going to go with Phil Capron. We did a deal where I was the key principal for the purchase. Phil is just tenacious; most operators would have given up on this deal, even though it was a great purchase. Phil just grinds away and makes it happen. Fearless. Very impressive. I am excited to do some more deals with him.

You are at a holiday party and asked what you do for a living. What do you say?

I generally say I work in tech, unless they are really interested, and then I usually say we own and manage multi-family real estate.

What is the best piece of investing advice that you've ever received?

Never fall in love with a property and make emotional decisions. There will always be another property. Slow down and make sure to spend the time on due diligence. Check zoning, talk to the city about outstanding violations, make very sure you understand the scope of the work the property will need.

What's your greatest alternative investment failure, and what would you do differently?

I would have gone bigger sooner: larger apartments and more of them. Until about six years ago, we did not use debt at all. I would have gone after 20- to 30-unit buildings in Oregon when I was going after 4- to 7-unit buildings. There is not much difference between the purchase and management of 30 versus 100 at the end of the day, but the scale of the financings and leverage is dramatically different.

In five years, do you still see yourself investing in this niche?

Absolutely! Most of the parks we have purchased will be seven to ten-year turnaround properties. At the end of that, I hope to have

ASK THE EXPERTS: Q&A With Jared Surnamer

Disclaimer: This Q&A is provided for informational purposes only. You should seek your own advice from professional advisors, including lawyers, financial advisors, and accountants, regarding the legal, tax, and financial implications of any investment you contemplate.

Jared Surnamer is founder of Valley Community Management, an umbrella management company. Growing up in a family of serial entrepreneurs, Jared was taught to see the world around him as an investment opportunity, a vision that truly shaped his early years. Since purchasing a large share of his family's manufactured housing holdings in 2015, he has grown to be a Top 100 operator in the nation by size in 2019, with continued expansion on the horizon.

When did you start investing?

I'm a small business guy. My parents owned a number of businesses throughout their careers—everything from manufacturing plants to travel agencies to accounting firms. So, from a young age, I was taught to think about investments. As a child, I "invested" in laser pointers and gumball machines. A friend and I bought it and supplied gumballs at the salon where my aunt cut hair. My mother would have to drive us to do refills. During my high school and university years, I started a web hosting businesses and event businesses. The types of investments have only gotten bigger and more complex since then!

To this day, I think about new areas of investment, revenue streams, and development. Investing and business development are areas that have always served as an outlet for my curiosity and creativity.

How were you introduced to mobile home parks?

Up until recently, people ended up working in some aspect of manufactured housing for one of two reasons: either they were born into it or they have some "funny story" that leads them down this path. In my case, it is the former. My parents purchased their first two communities in the late 1980s just before I was born. I literally grew up around manufactured housing. There are comical stories of me attending home showings as a little tyke with my mother and "helping out" in the office by banging away on the adding machine. I even have a namesake street in one of our communities. In 2015, I purchased a large share of their portfolio from them, which turned me into a rare breed of real estate investor: a second-generation manufactured housing community owner.

I chose this path because I believe it is an excellent asset class, and my deep knowledge of the industry gives me a leg up in the business. Today, this asset class is growing in popularity so I'm starting to see more folks coming into the industry because of diligent research, not just a "funny story" or family legacy.

What is the biggest negative you discovered?

Having grown up around the industry, I was well aware of the potential negatives that come with this type of niche asset class. Because manufactured housing has historically been a small subclass of residential rental real estate, there really wasn't a way to be "hands off" about the day-to-day aspects of the operation of the communities. When investing in apartments, you've got a massive number of resources at your fingertips. With manufactured housing, you have yourself, your wits, and your persistence. There are few informational resources available, and the industry is largely decentralized. There aren't third-party management companies with strong reputations for well-run communities. Staffing for a niche industry with a poor reputation is a challenge. Vendors for home transportation, installation, and utility operation are few and far between. Local zoning and municipalities might not support your business and residents. The list goes on, and I witnessed my parents go through most of this.

Family-operated communities were the only ones that seemed like they were well run, but this came at a cost. Growing up, every owner in our network lived with the fear that water would run out in their community. The phone would ring at any time of the day or night, and on the other side would be some kind of unforeseen emergency that needed to be dealt with immediately. My parents lived like this.

Nevertheless, I went through with the purchase because I believed I could scale the business, take advantage of new technology and the growing popularity of this asset class, build a management team, and ultimately not be tethered to my phone in fear of water leaks. I remember thinking, "Colonel Sanders isn't at every KFC!" As this industry evolves from mom-and-pop operators to national centralized operators, the entire asset class is becoming more formalized, and I believe this is a good thing for owners and residents.

What is your most memorable experience in this asset class?

There are many. Property management is a 24/7 job, and emergencies happen on their schedule—not yours. Furthermore, you're dealing with housing, one of the most intimate aspects of people's lives. Because of these two aspects of property management, you get a front row seat to both witness and mitigate the good, the bad, and the ugly of everyday existence.

The most memorable recent experience took place late last year. One Tuesday night, I received a call from the police about a house fire at one of the communities. I had just come home from playing tennis and was still wearing my workout gear. I was looking forward to sitting down with my wife and watching some TV, and I quickly realized I had to throw some sweats on top of my shorts, put my dinner in a Tupperware, and drive up to the property. For context, there have been plenty of other housefires, deaths, tornado evacuations, flooding, and the like in the past, and seldom do I show up on site while emergency personnel are there. These events are usually handled by my on-site teams.

I wasn't quite prepared for what I was about to witness at the property. This community is nearly a mile long, and all of the cul de sacs jut off of one, long, tree-lined boulevard. The fire department stopped me at the entrance and forbade passage until they realized that I was one of the owners. They then escorted me up the road to the house that was ablaze, past countless emergency vehicles and the crowds of residents that had started to congregate to see what all the commotion was about. There were at least 100 emergency personnel on site. The house fire was still raging, and residents were fearful for their safety. The police and fire department were keeping the crowds controlled, but there were some people live streaming the fire on Facebook. I found myself standing in the middle of an emotional mob of residents who were squarely placing the blame for the fire on management and demanding answers I couldn't really provide at that moment. Aware of the optics—the raging fire behind me and the Facebook feed—it was an excellent opportunity to practice detachment, compassion, and listening in order to address the group and keep everyone safe. I was forced to throw on my crisis management hat in a way that had never before been required.

Thankfully, no one was hurt and only one home was destroyed, but months later, we're still dealing with the aftermath of that fire.

What is a common misconception about mobile home parks?

I sometimes hear that the management of MH communities is easier than the management of apartments. I've managed both multi-family units and MH communities during my brief career, and based on this experience, I conclude that this assertion is probably not true. Managing MH communities can be more complicated than apartments because of the specialized labor and project management that is required to keep the community running smoothly.

Assuming that your communities are all homeowner-occupied, then there can be some occupancy and maintenance benefits for management. For example, my average tenancy is well over ten years, so I'm not chasing after annual renewals. Likewise, I don't get calls about leaky toilets because homeowners are responsible for the maintenance of their homes. However, from a management perspective, I think the benefits of MH over apartments stop there. Third-party management is rarely an option for MH communities, and the economics of a property mean that unless you have a substantially sized property (over 150 units), you have to find very cost-effective labor. Cost-effective often translates into on-the-job training and staff that requires quite a bit of oversight. Your property manager must be a miniature CEO with excellent project management skills. You may have water wells and wastewater treatment plants that need to be maintained under the very strict regulations of the DEP. That means you (or a member of your team) have to learn how to operate and repair these systems, conduct daily water tests, and submit reports.

The alternative is that you pay a third-party operator a pretty hefty fee to keep your facility up to code and your property out of the crosshairs of regulators. Aside from operating the system, your maintenance team needs to know how to locate and repair underground water or sewer leaks, which is usually out of the scope of many cost-effective laborers. You also have some asset-specific parts of the business, such as ordering and bringing in new homes. This requires selecting a floor plan that will sell in your market, placing the order with the factory, securing building permits, preparing the homesite, upgrading utility lines, coordinating with transportation and installers.

This one aspect of operating MH communities could be a discipline and business unto itself, yet it is absolutely required for keeping your property full and occupied. This is so much more complicated than hiring a few guys to throw on a new coat of paint and replace carpeting in an apartment unit in order to get it ready for market.

What is the most important thing an investor should know when considering a mobile home park?

Assuming you have taken adequate time to investigate deal killer due diligence items—working utilities, being able to legally operate, no environmental disasters, and so on—the next most important question to investigate is whether or not your market will support the sale of new homes. Even if your model assumptions are off, or if you missed a major capital improvement in your analysis, if you can sell new homes, you will be able to weather any storm. Sure, maybe your ROI will be off for the year. But if you can sell a new home, that means you have a repeatable model that will bring in a strong new tenant, upgrade the look of the community, and that you have sufficient demand in your area that renting homes can be a very strong Plan B or C.

What is your professional background, and how did it affect your investing career?

Though I grew up in this industry, I believe that my academic study at NYU's Stern School of Business helped prepare me for expansion and breaking out of the shell of a mom-and-pop operator mindset. I had a double major in accounting and management, and while they are helpful theories and subjects, I don't think they are necessary for success in the field.

What information sources have been the most influential for you?

In an age where everyone with a mic and a social media channel deems themselves an expert, there's a lot of unvetted advice out there. The industry is rife with purveyors of "get rich quick" business plans, so it can be hard to come by tried-and-true references for the daily operation of this business and for investment strategy. After all, this is the second youngest real estate asset class, so there's much that hasn't been documented, and the industry is in the midst of an evolution/consolidation. A lot of what I know about the operation of manufactured housing communities has been garnered through a mix of hard learned trial and error, alongside having grown up in the industry.

From the investment point of view, Frank Rolfe's Mobile Home University Bootcamp was the most comprehensive educational product I participated in. His experience of having gone through the ups and downs of investment is evident in his content. It was an eye opener for me. As a mom-and-pop operator, I never dreamed you could manage communities from afar. The framework of remote management was totally outside of the mom-and-pop ethos that I had been raised on. Rolfe has a lot of great content and, as a whole, it provides the best summary I have seen related to owning, operating, and investing in MH communities. Having attended his bootcamp with a background in the industry, I could verify through firsthand experience that he wasn't making stuff up. Rolfe runs a podcast, and many more have popped up. For my personal use, the content on these podcasts come across as repetitive, but I do believe it would be particularly useful for someone who is new to the industry.

I haven't read a business book in years. One of the first books I read on real estate was The Real Estate Game *by William Poorvu. It helped me understand why real estate is a good business to be in. I tend to lean toward self-help or philosophy books for personal reading. Information is the food of your brain. Just like my food diet, I try to keep my information sources varied.*

Who that you personally know do you most respect in business, and why?

I have a partner in one community named Doug. I respect him immensely because he hasn't let the temptation of financial success disrupt his sense of contentment. Despite his financial achievements, Doug, in my opinion, leads a balanced and ethical life. I've negotiated with him on both sides of the table, and it is evident that what matters most to Doug during his business dealings is whether something is the correct, ethical course of action. His mindset would not allow for greed or complaining. He is also a great husband and father, as evidenced by his warm, loving family.

I've heard it phrased that your success is largely determined by what you are willing to sacrifice. If you're willing to sacrifice TV watching to instead practice piano, you are more likely to succeed in piano. I know many people who have sacrificed their ethics or their relationships with their kids or partners in the name of making a lot of money. To me, that is not success. It is easier to shut out the immaterial things in life and focus on something like accumulating wealth. It is much harder to remain balanced and not lose sight of finance, ethics, and relationships while experiencing success in all three areas. Thrice divorced, severed personal relationships, no concern for your health, and a big bank account? That isn't an impressive report card for success, in my opinion. It is simply evidence of questionable trades and sacrifices. To say you want to do well, be there for your family, and not trample others—now that is ambition.

You are at a holiday party and asked what you do for a living. What do you say?

I own and operate mobile home parks. If I say I operate manufactured housing communities, they tend to gloss over.

What is the best piece of investing advice that you've ever received?

Well, let me start with the best piece of investment advice I've ever heard, from none other than Warren Buffet: "Risk comes from not knowing what you're doing." Specific to this niche, however, the best advice relates to a previous response: "Sales is the lifeblood of the business." Traditional mom-and-pop wisdom will tell you that the whole business is in space rent. Don't worry about making money on the sale or anything else. If the sites are full and paying, you can weather just about any storm. The prerequisite to a full community is the ability to sell a home on site.

What's your greatest alternative investment failure, and what would you do differently?

I walked away from a deal because, while on site during a due diligence septic inspection, the septic technician said, "If I were you, I'd run!" In the follow up, the company said they could not quote the total repair on the septic issue without doing some expensive testing. I was nervous, so I countered with the worst-case scenario and offered the seller several hundred thousand dollars less than the asking price. This was naive and an awful idea. First, septic technicians and the companies they work for are in the business of finding all possible liabilities. The business decisions are the job of the investor. Second, I found out that the buyer who came in after me got a $70,000 credit, and the total repair job was about $125,000. The property was so under market that by raising the rents to market norms, the new buyers created at least $600,000–700,000 in value.

In a nutshell, I got nervous, got tight with due diligence dollars, and didn't explore every possible option to make the deal work. I lost out on a lot of upside because of that.

In five years, do you still see yourself investing in this niche?

Definitely. The economics are excellent, and affordable housing will always be an important need in the country.

TAKEAWAYS

- Huge tailwinds with affordable housing in incredible demand
- Most affordable way to purchase a starter home
- Negative stigma of the "trailer park" is slow to change
- Operations is often overlooked by new investors
- Huge percentage of parks still owned by mom-and-pop sellers
- Seller financing is more readily available in this space
- More value-add deals in this space from retired owners
- Very few new parks built create monopolies for existing parks

---

8
SELF-STORAGE

"People don't get rid of stuff."
—Kris Benson, Chief Investment Officer, Reliant Real Estate
Management

I was born in 1987. During my lifetime, the percentage of the U.S. population that uses self-storage has grown from less than 3% to 8%[26]. That's a 166.67% increase! This is a mind-blowing number when you consider that according to the U.S. Census, the population in the United States increased only 35%—from 242.3 million to 327.2 million—during the same time period. Can you imagine the sheer volume of "stuff" that is being stored to justify these numbers?

Now look at those numbers in a different way: How would you like to profit from a customer base that totals over 26 million people? If that was the population of a state, it would be right behind Texas as the third largest in the United States!

When I first started doing my due diligence about investing in self-storage, the one thing that I found fascinating is how complementary storage space is to commercial real estate.

---

[26] Self-Storage Almanac. Phoenix, AZ: MiniCo, 2020-2021.

Everything that can be a negative for an apartment building operator is somewhat of a positive for self-storage. This is illustrated by what is commonly known in the self-storage industry as the "4 D's of life": death, divorce, downsizing, and dislocation. As an apartment building operator, those are words you rarely want to hear from your tenants, but they are music to the ears of a self-storage operator because they all cause a huge surge in demand for the asset. It's no wonder that self-storage has performed extremely well during the tumultuous times caused by the last two economic recessions.

The self-storage industry is in a very transitional time period with new specialty applications—including climate-controlled lockers and wine storage space—being developed on a continuous basis. Here are a few other unorthodox examples that come to mind; they illustrate how operators whose background is not in self-storage have added complementary storage space to their other investments, increasing NOI and investor returns substantially:

- An operator converted old, abandoned malls into huge, profitable self-storage facilities.
- A residential operator retrofitted unlivable basement space across 20 apartment buildings with rentable storage lockers.
- A retail strip operator converted half of his storage into one self-storage facility. His occupancy increased to over 90%.
- A mobile home park operator added a mini self-storage site on empty land in the park that would not have been able to support additional homes due to zoning laws.

I'm sure this is just the start of the offshoots that will be developed in this explosive industry. At the end of the day, all you need for a self-storage facility is empty land or a vacant building that can be retrofitted.

What Is the Asset?

Self-storage, also known as self-service storage, consists of physical space (such as rooms, lockers, containers, or garages) that can be rented out to individuals or businesses on a month-to-month basis. While longer leases are sometimes available, they are not the industry norm.

The cost to build a new self-storage facility is considerably less per square foot than other real estate asset classes because it requires less infrastructure, such as plumbing, electric, and other systems and fixtures that are not required. In general, most other expenses are fixed, and only a small staff is required to run an individual facility, keeping operational expenses low. This model lends itself well to producing a heavy cash flow stream for its investors.

The self-storage model offers opportunities to cross market similar high-profit margin items, such as packaging supplies, insurance, and moving trucks. In fact, you almost always see a few U-Hauls® in every self-storage facility you drive by. If you don't, you may have just identified an easy way to bring up the NOI for the facility. In my neighborhood, there are actually U-Haul® self-storage facilities going up. I guess everyone wants to get in on the action.

The units themselves are usually secured by the tenants' own locks, but the facility may provide additional security in the form of gated entries and cameras. The storage facility is typically not liable for any theft or damage of the items in storage, but as mentioned previously, operators usually offer insurance to tenants to cover the contents of their unit.

In the case of tenant delinquencies, an operator can place a lien on the stored goods and retain a third-party auctioneer to sell the items and recoup past-due rent. The time frame for this is dictated by the terms of the lease and the lien laws in the state in which the unit is located.

What Is the History of the Asset?

The first storage facility chain opened up in Texas in the 1960s. The Lone Star State had a huge and growing demand for residents needing a place to store their personal belongings since most homes are not built with basements.[27] The original concept was simple: Find low-cost real estate on the outer edges of the city, and place prefabricated garages there for rent. The original operators had no clue how much pent-up demand they were tapping into, but the idea took off in a "if you build it, they will come" scenario: As the garages began to fill up, other operators began copying the model, and the business concept began to take off like wildfire in the 1970s. While the exact reason for the explosive growth is unknown, many industry experts attribute it to the following events:

- The rise of the global economy triggering an over-accumulation crisis. Overaccumulation is the point where

[27] Tom Vanderbilt, "Self-storage nation," *Slate Magazine* (July 18, 2005), https://slate.com/culture/2005/07/self-storage-in-america.html.

reinvestment of capital no longer produces any additional returns. The occurs when the market is inundated with capital, resulting in extensive devaluation.

- The beginning of the migration from northern cities to the cheaper Sunbelt
- The introduction and rise of no-fault divorces

What Are the Current Regulations on Buying and Selling the Asset?

From an operator's perspective, a self-storage facility has to be compliant with its state laws, which are actually very friendly toward the industry. This includes laws that allow for reasonable late fees to be charged without risking potential litigation.[28] A few states also charge a state sales tax on the rents charged. From an asset perspective, the regulations are lighter than what you would see in other asset classes mainly because the leases are month to month, and there's nothing stopping the consumer from leaving at the end of each month.

Unlike mobile home parks, towns readily approve new self-storage facilities, and given the low cost per square foot to build combined with the high market demand, new facilities have been going up like wildfire. It's no surprise then that, in the last five years, there has been a greater new supply of rentable space than in the prior 50 years combined.

---

[28] "An overview of self-storage law," Inside Self-Storage, March 1, 2005, https://www.insideselfstorage.com/archive/overview-self-storage-law.

What Is the Market for the Asset?

From an operator's perspective, self-storage is very much a micro market game. The thing that matters most is looking at the 1-, 3-, and 5-mile radius demographics; roughly 70% of your customers will come from between 3–5 miles from your facility. This is in contrast to other commercial real estate, where the demographics of the entire markets plays a major role. One reason for this is because of how saturated most markets typically are for new self-storage. Most likely, if your radius is too large, you will have encroached on a competitor's facility.

From an acquisition perspective, over 52% of facilities are owned by "mom and pop" operators.[29] In fact, besides mobile home parks, there are very few asset classes that still have such a large number of small-scale operators—many of which are looking to retire and avoid big overhauls of systems and property renovations. There may also be an opportunity to obtain owner financing since most retiring owners are looking for a steady cash flow in their retirement. Besides owner financing, self-storage facilities are one of the real estate plays that qualify for SBA loans, which allows them to be purchased for as little as 10% down.

From an investor's perspective, most operators in this space offer opportunities to invest in a fund or individual deals, but they do require accredited status.

---

[29] Self-Storage Almanac. Phoenix, AZ: MiniCo, 2020-2021.

It's worth noting that through diligent networking, you may be able to find joint venture deals where accreditation is not needed, but they would require you to have an active role in the project, which might be too much of a time commitment when starting out. The topic of joint ventures in real estate could fill its own book, but it's not one that I would recommend for a new investor. As a general rule, you should be familiar with the space and possibly have already invested in a few deals as a limited partner before entertaining joint ventures.

The Bad Apples: Has Anybody Committed Fraud in This Asset class?

Not necessarily. But there are several misconceptions that exist out there when it comes to investing in self-storage. First, some investors have a tough time rationalizing investing in self-storage when they personally don't use such facilities. This is also the case when it comes to investing in ATMs (Chapter 10). However, the statistics supporting self-storage usage are undeniable.

Second, some investors believe that self-storage facilities are easy to operate. It's true that when a tenant leaves, the operator can just sweep out the unit and turn it over to a new tenant—plus, they don't have to deal with leaking toilets. While the maintenance aspect of the facilities is minimal, the operational requirements of the business are high. Tenants leave more often because they are on month-to-month leases. This requires aggressive marketing plans and excellent customer service initiatives that can be measured. Everything from the logo to the telephone greeting needs to be systemized—and all of this adds up to needing an experienced operator.

What Are the Lessons to Be Learned?

Don't jump headfirst into this asset class thinking it's easy. Like many alternative investments, the best way to get started is with a fund or investing as a limited partner on a syndication. When you do invest, make sure you look at the team behind the deal and the systems they have in place—not just the numbers.

The best way to source operators that specialize in self-storage is— you guessed it—network, network, network! BiggerPockets is a great resource for sourcing recommendations. Also, reading self-storage publications like the *Self-Storage Almanac* will help you become more familiar with different markets. Also, consider going to the Inside Self-Storage World Expo,[30] a three-day, non-stop industry networking event where you can meet self-storage owners, managers, developers, and other investors. If this doesn't sound like fun, keep in mind that the 2021 event is in Las Vegas. A trip might cost you $5,000, which is a lot of money, but not when you consider that the minimum investment for a syndication is ten times that amount. Between the networking and the knowledge gained from industry experts, the returns are exponentially higher than the initial cost.

The Pros and Cons of Self-Storage Investing

PROS

- Asset class performed extremely well in the last two recessions
- Demand statistics are trending upward
- Over 52% of self-storage facilities are still owned by mom-and-pop sellers

---

[30] https://www.issworldexpo.com/en/home.html

- Month-to-month leases allow for quicker rent increases
- SBA loans make it possible to purchase a self-storage facility with as little at 10% down
- Low maintenance
- Healthy cash flow business
- Construction cost per square foot is lower than other real estate
- Lower operational expenses
- Can be added on to other business models, such as mobile home parks or apartment buildings, to increase NOI
- High-profit auxiliary items, like moving trucks and packaging supplies, are easy upsells
- Very complementary to other asset classes in commercial real estate

CONS
- More supply in the last five years than in the entire history of the asset
- Very low barriers for competitors in your geographic area
- Your competition might be a well-funded REIT
- Month-to-month leases lead to high turnover
- Intense marketing and operational requirements

ASK THE EXPERTS: Q&A With Taylor Loht

Disclaimer: This Q&A is provided for informational purposes only. You should seek your own advice from professional advisors, including lawyers, financial advisors, and accountants, regarding the legal, tax, and financial implications of any investment you contemplate.

Taylor Loht is a real estate syndicator, passive investor in syndications, and host of the Passive Wealth Strategy Show. *He actively syndicates workforce multi-family housing, and—because he's a fan of diversification—also holds passive investments in syndicated self-storage.*

When did you start investing?

I first started investing when I graduated from college. Finally having two nickels to rub together, I picked up a copy of Benjamin Graham's The Intelligent Investor. *This book turned me into a value investor from Day 1, when I began investing in value stocks.*

Years later, I learned of the value of cash-flowing real estate from a little purple book you've probably heard of before – Rich Dad Poor Dad. *That hit me at a critical time, when I was deep in the process of returning to school for an MBA and career change. I changed my investment strategy, and indeed my philosophy about money, and invested in my first apartment complexes in late 2016.*

How were you introduced to self-storage?

Through a podcast, early in the podcasting days. If you're not listening to real estate investing podcasts, you most certainly should be. You are the average of the five people you spend the most time with. Many busy professionals, in my estimation, spend far too much time with newscasters and talking heads on television. Their wealth, health, and happiness would greatly benefit from spending more time with thought leaders on constructive podcasts.

What is the biggest negative you discovered?

Illiquidity and the life span of a larger real estate investment is not ideal for some. At the time of this writing, the self-storage property I'm invested in has a ten-year business plan. Ten years! That's not for the faint of heart. I still went forward with it because included in that ten-year time projection is cash flow. I get to benefit from income the property generates while we own it.

What is your most memorable experience in this asset class?

On the positive side, I love seeing new buildings go up. I haven't had a negative experience yet. That's not to say there aren't negative experiences to be had because there certainly are. I do my best to mitigate that through conservative investing and very careful partnering.

What is a common misconception about self-storage?

We sometimes hear that there are no deals to be had, or that the REITs and big box guys have flooded the market. That is certainly true in some areas, including primary markets. Smaller markets still have untapped demand and poorly managed properties for enterprising investors to buy and improve!

What is the most important thing an investor should know when considering self-storage?

For any type of real estate investment, the market and location of the property are always the biggest factors to start with. In self-storage investing, we look at supply and demand in the market.

Many primary markets are overbuilt, or at least very hard for non-REIT investors to compete in.

What is your professional background, and how did it affect your investing career?

My professional background is in sales and engineering. I attended the University of Delaware for Chemical Engineering, and I am confident that education helped immensely. Engineering work and education teach you how to break a problem down into components and work through each one step by step.

What information sources have been the most influential for you?

Outside of real estate, I love the James Altucher Show. James is an eccentric guy with a successful track record in hedge funds, venture capital, angel investing, and technology. He has a fantastic track record of being on the cusp of changing industries and technologies.

Who that you personally know do you most respect in business, and why?

I know so many people I respect. One who I'm happy to call a friend is Whitney Sewell. He's on a mission to support adoptions, and he is doing a fantastic job. He saw a change he wanted to make in the world, saw a way to get there through real estate syndication, and pulled out all the stops in his pursuit of that goal.

I first met Whitney before he got into real estate syndication, right when he joined our coaching group. He told me about his mission and everything in his life he was changing to achieve that goal. Since then, he has built a fantastic syndication business, supported his mission, helped his passive investors earn great returns, and shown us all the power of commitment, drive, and purpose. Win-win-win-win!

You are at a holiday party and asked what you do for a living. What do you say?

"I buy real estate with passive investors and split the return"—the same way I explain real estate syndication on my show.

What is the best piece of investing advice that you've ever received?

Your network is your net worth. Many of these deals happen pretty quietly: off-market transactions, non-marketed equity raises, and the like. The stronger relationships you have, the more opportunities you'll get.

What's your greatest alternative investment failure, and what would you do differently?

Losing time or sitting on the sidelines. Action is always better than inaction. Earl Nightingale, a speaker who was essentially the mid-20th century's Tony Robbins, said, "Success is the progressive realization of a worthy goal."

In five years, do you still see yourself investing in this niche?

Absolutely. I'm in it for the long haul. In five years, we will have even better tools and technologies to deploy to improve operations and grow our revenues.

ASK THE EXPERTS: Q&A With Kris Benson

Disclaimer: This Q&A is provided for informational purposes only. You should seek your own advice from professional advisors, including lawyers, financial advisors, and accountants, regarding the legal, tax, and financial implications of any investment you contemplate.

As Chief Investment Officer of Reliant Real Estate Management, Kris Benson oversees the equity-raising arm of the firm, sits on the investment committee, and manages investor relations. In the past 24 months, the Reliant team has been responsible for over $200 million in self-storage acquisition across the southeastern United States. In addition to deep experience as an executive sales professional, Kris brings a wealth of knowledge from his ownership experience in the commercial multi-family arena. Kris lives with his wife and children in Roswell, GA.

When did you start investing?

I started investing during my first college internship at NorthWestern Mutual. I bought several variable universal life policies, which I later surrendered for various reasons. I subsequently started investing in stocks after graduating college and opening a 401(k) plan.

How were you introduced to self-storage?

My story is somewhat unique. I started as a residential real estate investor buying duplexes in the town I lived in. I did that for a while until I realized it wouldn't be scalable. I then transitioned to large multi-family apartments. A quote that comes to mind when I started scaling up was "big deals and small deals are the same amount of work; you just make less money on small deals." Shortly after the transition, we sold off our smaller residential portfolio and started developing a 64-unit residential complex. We also started investing in passive syndications across the United States. When we started operating at scale, we had the lightbulb moment that this was how to make money in commercial real estate.

About five years ago, I wanted to diversify into an additional asset class. I identified the self-storage space and met with a number of different operators looking for the right fit. I had a group of investors that invested alongside of me, making it more attractive for the operator than if it was just my capital. That's how I met my current operator. I started as an investor and was later asked to join the operational team.

What is the biggest negative you discovered?

The biggest negative in self-storage is the unheralded amount of new supply that has come online in the last five years. For a frame of reference, since 2018, the self-storage industry delivered more new rentable square footage than the entire history of the asset

189

class combined. The reason for this surge of new supply is that the asset has performed remarkably well during the last two market meltdowns (2008 and 2020).

The reason that I still went through with the investment is that the oversupply was focused on the top 50 (primary) real estate markets in the country. The operator I ended up investing with had a market focus of secondary and tertiary markets. Even in the last few years, we have been transitioning even more into the tertiary space.

What is your most memorable experience in this asset class?

While I can't pinpoint one exact experience, what has amazed me is that people don't like to get rid of stuff. I can't tell you how many times I have been in units where cars were rotting into the ground, but people were paying to basically store rust. Other times, the storage unit contents were not actually worth one month's worth of rent, yet the person paid for three years to store the contents. I think the value placed on "stuff" in America is the reason why the industry exists. For someone who is new to the industry, they may be shocked at the demand for the units. Currently 1 out of 9 Americans use self-storage. It is very much a "build and they will come" moment in the industry.

What is a common misconception about self-storage?

Investors go into the investment thinking it's going to be easier than other asset classes that they have invested in since units can be turned over with a quick sweep, and the ongoing maintenance is usually minor since there's no toilets, plumbing, or appliances to worry about. While there is definitely a component to that, self-

storage is much more of an operational business wrapped around real estate. Leases are usually month to month, so the customer turnover is much more frequent than what you would see in a typical 12-month lease. This is a double-edged sword since you can raise rent quicker, but you can also lose tenants just as fast. So there is a huge component involving customer service, marketing, etc., that you wouldn't find in other real estate assets.

It's not uncommon for me to run into a new investor in the space who thinks they could purchase their own self-storage and run it as a passive investor without an infrastructure in place. It's not a passive investment without the systems, and even then, it takes a team.

What is the most important thing an investor should know when considering self-storage?

Generally, as a passive investor, you are making a bet on an operator. If something goes wrong, unless it's fraudulent, the limited partner has very little recourse, and the only variable that can save the deal is an experienced operating team. The team is going to make or break the deal, and this is true in every asset class—not just in the self-storage space. The deal is important, but not as important as a relevant track record of the operator. It doesn't help the investor if the operator had a long track record in the industrial space but is now raising funds for an apartment building. Having a deep understanding of the operator's track record is probably the best indicator of how your deal will perform. But keep in mind how value was created on prior deals: Was the deal just a lucky participant in cap rates compressing, or were the actions of the operating team responsible for the value created?

What is your professional background, and how did it help you in your investing career?

My professional background was in surgical sales, which means I have no problems with talking to almost anybody. The ability to go out and "bird dog" allowed me to apply those skills in finding real estate opportunities. I think the key, regardless if you are a passive or active investor, is to jump in. You have to do something, or you're going to analyze for the next five years and not do anything. There's a quote that I really love by Winston Churchill: "Perfection is the enemy of progress." Some people want to learn everything before making a decision. I am not saying to invest in something that you don't understand, but the true learning happens when you're in a deal. My career set me up with the ability to say, "I want to learn how that happens, and I am going to call enough people in that space until I feel comfortable with my grasp of how it happens."

What information sources have been the most influential for you?

When the BiggerPockets podcast started, it really opened my horizons to investing in different real estate deals, and it was very influential to me. It was great to be a participant on the podcast later on too.

The book Rich Dad Poor Dad really struck me when I read it in my early 20s. It went against the grain of the people advising me at the time to go to school, get a job, make as much money as you can. I was fortunate to do that, but making money didn't make me happy. I then realized it's not the money; it's what the money can buy you, which is freedom. That's important. The book changed my perspective. It made me realize it wasn't about how much I was *making, as long as it was creating that freedom for me. I hope to pass this mindset on to my two children. I even paid them to read* Rich Dad Poor Dad *because I wanted it to be ingrained into their mindset. It's something that I wish I had in my earlier years.*

Who that you personally know do you most respect in business, and why?

One of my original real estate mentors. I am omitting his name because he might feel uncomfortable with me mentioning him, but I am glad to go over the "why," which I think is even more important. He was a developer for 30-plus years, and he's extremely wise and patient. What I admire about him is that he is always willing to share his 30 years of experience in order to make sure I don't make the same mistakes he once did, and that has been so valuable in my career that there is no way I would have been able to replicate my success without knowing him. In his industry, he's extremely well-respected for his integrity and willingness to help others. He willingly mentors others, even though his time is scarce. Whenever I refer anyone to him, I get the happiest follow-up calls about the referrals.

You are at a holiday party and asked what you do for a living. What do you say?

We provide institutional-quality investments in self-storage properties for accredited investors. Usually, people respond by saying that they have seen those things going up all over the place.

What is the best piece of investing advice that you've ever received?

Understand the market story and how to evaluate a market. What I mean by that is that self-storage is very much a micro-market game. The only thing that matters is the 1-, 3-, and 5-mile radius. Sometimes, the rural areas have a larger radius, but generally, 70% of your customers are coming from that 3- to 5-mile radius. You really have to understand the story of that micro market. What's happening at the metropolitan statistical area (MSA) level doesn't matter. For example, if Charlotte, NC, is having a 20% population boom, but the 3- to 5-mile radius near your self-storage is deteriorating, the MSA's impact will be irrelevant.

We try to understand the story of a particular market. The story is not dictated by one single metric, like population growth, job growth, traffic count, or average square foot per person. It's understanding all of those things and listening to the story the market is telling you. It is very much an art and not a science, and that's partially because it's not a mature asset class like multi-family. There are not as robust data sets as multi-family because, until recently, it was a very niche space. It only became a "real" asset class in the last decade or so.

What's your greatest alternative investment failure, and what would you do differently?

Trying to time the market at a macro level. I have tried in equities and in real estate, and it generally worked out pretty poorly for me.

In five years, do you still see yourself investing in this niche?

Yes, absolutely. My personal belief is that due to interest rate compression, more and more money will chase hard assets like real estate because there is little yield from treasuries. The bigger capital players, like life insurance companies and pensions, have liabilities and have to deploy capital. If there is no yield to be had with more conservative investments, the investments will flow toward real assets like self-storage because there's still yield to be found. For our company, our strategy is to continue to create value for our investors by building an institutional-quality portfolio and evaluating disposition opportunities based on the market conditions.

TAKEAWAYS

- Abundant new supply being built in recent years
- Very low cost of entry for new facilities
- Operations overlooked by newer operators
- Great tools for apartment building and mobile home park operators to increase NOI
- 1-, 3-, 5-mile demographic critical to understanding the market for an investment
- Large share of mom-and-pop sellers

9
MULTI-ASSET FUNDS

Introduction written by Mark Cira, Founder of Cira Capital Group

I intended on writing the introduction to every chapter in this book myself, but when I was going through Mark's words looking for the perfect quote to use as an opening line, I couldn't figure out where to stop because I liked each new line more than the previous one. This is not a surprise if you know Mark and how caring and knowledgeable he is about his real estate, his business partners, and his family. I hope you enjoy his introduction as much as I do.

Multi-asset funds are some of the most attractive private real estate investments because they allow you to achieve some degree of diversification with a modest investment. A strategic investment in a variety of funds can get you diversification across a variety of asset types, classes, geographies, and operators. And consistent investment over many years will provide diversification across time, and investment cycles. All of these actions significantly reduce your portfolio risk and its exposure to any single asset, class, region, operator, or cycle. However, unless you have significant wealth that you can spread across a variety of fund operators, your portfolio will still face a fair amount of operator risk.

Although diversification is a laudable goal and one of the key strategies fund managers employ in creating sustained returns, the reality is that it is difficult to achieve unless you're already quite wealthy. The unfortunate reality is that only about 10% or fewer Americans have enough wealth to adequately diversify their private real estate portfolio. Unlike the stock market, where you can easily diversify by spreading money across index funds or simply buying small amounts of shares in companies that may cost anywhere from a few dollars to a few hundred dollars, you can't do that very effectively with private real estate. That's because minimums in private real estate investments with reputable operators typically start at $25,000, and many funds have minimums in the $50,000–$100,000 range. It's rare to find quality investments or operators who will accept smaller investment increments. That's why it generally takes significant net worth—often $1 million or more—to adequately diversify a private real estate portfolio.

What Is the Asset?
A multi-asset fund is exactly what it sounds like: a fund that includes a variety of different investment types that are typically related in some way. It can also consist of just one asset class, such as residential apartments, but with multiple apartment buildings in one portfolio, as opposed to just one.

As we go through various asset classes in this book, you're probably noticing that sometimes their pros and cons overlap; in some cases, they complement each other, while in others, they don't. For example, there are some prominent multi-asset funds that include only mobile home parks (Chapter 7) and self-storage (Chapter 8). If you look at their respective chapters in this book, there is some clear crossover: Both asset classes have attracted a surge of investor interest during the last decade; both involve a majority of mom-and-pop sellers with the potential for seller financing; and both usually provide immediate opportunity to improve the NOI due to neglected maintenance and operations. As a result, it makes sense for those two assets to be combined in the same fund. Furthermore, this type of pairing allows the fund operator to choose from among a wider spectrum of opportunities, improving their ability to find the best matches for a specific portfolio.

Note: While most of the deals discussed in this chapter center around real estate, there are a wide range of assets that can be combined in a multi-asset fund model. However, I would instantly be leery of any fund that invests in assets between which you can't draw any parallels. Case in point: The cryptocurrency theme is everywhere these days, but that doesn't mean I want to invest in a fund that somehow ties in bitcoins to apartment buildings, or vice versa. Likewise, I once looked at a real estate investment deal for what I originally thought was a single property. I liked the operator and the model, but somewhere in the middle of his presentation, the operator started describing a multi-asset fund that was implementing hedges on commodities that somehow tied back to the performance of the property. I didn't have to look at another slide after that to say no to do the deal. Sometimes, it really is that simple.

Multi-asset funds are commonly called "blind funds." The reason is because at the time of the initial capital raise, the assets have not yet been purchased. The criteria for the assets are known based on the operator's track record, but the operator waits until they have cash on hand—or, at the very least, cash commitments have been made—before entering into a contract. This is a common practice since operators pay a lot of money out of pocket for the initial due diligence processes associated with getting a property under contract. As the fund ages (over a period of months or even years), investors have better access to information that helps them decide if the fund is right for them.

Keep in mind that it's not uncommon for a new fund to wait six months or more to start paying out after the initial launch. Even though early investors continue to earn the accrued preferred distribution during this period, most investors prefer to shorten the period between investment and distribution whenever possible— especially in the case of an income fund.

> **PRO TIP**: *In my opinion, it's usually better to invest in a fund closer to its closing than when it first opens, as long as you can accept the possibility of not receiving an allocation if the shares sell out. The reason to invest later is to allow the portfolio to become seasoned so distributions can begin sooner. The risk of being sold out is real, but usually you would receive multiple notifications prior to the fund closing its doors to new investors.*

For a growth fund, timing the fund investment is a moot point because the business model is so dramatically different. Operators are aware of this, so they usually incentivize early investors with slightly better rates and guaranteed allocations. While my personal preference is to wait, some strong operators rarely have open funds, and the risk of not getting an allocation isn't worth the delay in some cases.

There are two main types of multi-asset funds:

1. **Classic fund manager model** — In this traditional model, operators usually have an extensive background in the asset classes in which they specialize. For example, a fund manager in the apartment building space may have been an operator for many years. This expertise gives them an advantage in being able to identify other competent operators. While the fund manager relies on his network and experience to allocate investor money, this is a lot less time consuming than personally operating the individual assets.

2. **Operators raising funds for their own deals** — In reality, this increasingly popular approach is just like other syndications that we have discussed in previous chapters, but with considerable added scale and flexibility for the operator. The reasons for using this model vary. Sometimes operators want to have ample capital on hand to seize another opportunity on the horizon or to smooth out some of the peaks and valleys in their capital-raising process. To be certain, there are times when operators get inundated with investor money, and other times when there are so many competing deals being presented simultaneously to the investor community that attracting funding becomes very difficult.

Case in point: In Fall 2020, four operators in my network were presenting deals at the same time. As a result of the increased competition, the capital-raising period lasted twice as long as it would have otherwise, and a few strong operators raised until the last possible moment to get their deals done. You can think of the ideal approach to timing as being similar to the way box office movies are scheduled for release by their production houses. For obvious reasons, these companies avoid debuting their movies on the same date that a big premiere like *Star Wars* is due in theaters. Under the fund model, even if there was a conflict in timing, an operator would have pre-sold their "tickets" beforehand or at least received a considerable down payment for the project. I foresee the fund trend continuing to pick up steam among operators as we move into the future.

In either scenario, an investor should take a close look at the fund's track record. The fund will usually be labeled with a number in the title, such as Income Fund 7. This means that this is the seventh fund that the manager has operated using roughly the same business model. How can you tell it's the same business model? Usually, each model has its own fund name (i.e., Growth Appreciation 4 would be the fourth fund in a growth-focused business model, or heavy value-add deal).

Your due diligence should include requesting the operator's investor documents, which should detail the returns produced by their previous income funds. Word to the wise: Most operators with excellent track records will proudly promote them in these documents. While not a deal breaker, an omission of the track record should raise a red flag—and a refusal to provide the information indicates that it's a good time to walk away from the deal.

Keep in mind that when you invest in a multi-asset fund, you indirectly invest in the entire portfolio of the fund. I have invested in funds that contain only two assets, and I have invested in others with hundreds of assets, and the difference in volume usually derives from whether or not the fund is operating its own deals or not. A non-operating fund is typically a one-stop shop for diversification, but it gives up control over the performance of the individual deals. Because it has more projects, a non-operating fund tends to be invested in deals with a more diverse geographic footprint and a more varied timeline, with different deals being invested in and sold at staggered times. This provides some margin of safety for investors in the event that the fund manager invested at the peak of the market. Because of all of these moving parts, the related fees can get complicated, including an asset management fee, an investment placement fee, and a portion of the profit. But, to be fair, these are many of the same fees a regular syndicator charges for single deals.

Smaller funds—those that invest in fewer deals—operate the individual projects and have complete control over the performance of the individual deals. The fee structure is much simpler and usually mirrors a typical syndication. And as an investor, it's obviously easier to perform due diligence on a handful of deals, as opposed to hundreds of deals.

In the end, each model has its pros and cons, and each will fit into your portfolio differently, even though they are both classified as multi-asset funds.

What Is the History of the Asset?
The history of the asset class is directly correlated to the history of apartment building syndication. The JOBS Act of 2012 opened the doors for these types of funds to the average accredited investor.

What Are the Current Regulations on Buying and Selling the Asset?
Almost every multi-asset fund is a 506(c) Regulation D fund geared toward accredited investors. The reason is simple: If you are not accredited and invest in a multi-asset fund, that fund manager can no longer invest in any 506(c) deals. That would add unnecessary hardship to the already difficult job of sourcing quality deals.

What Is the Market for the Asset?
Similar to apartment building syndications, these assets are highly illiquid. The language in the investment documents clearly states that you will not be able to sell your investment in this security. If you do find yourself needing to get out of a situation that you did not foresee, expect a loss on some of the principal you invested. In the next decade or so, I predict that a secondary market will come

into focus for private securities. There are already one or two startups that are currently brokering larger deals. It has a long way to go, but it's a start.

The bright side is that if you invest in a few good multi-asset funds that are highly diversified, you can effectively take care of the right side of your alternative investment "pie" (as discussed in Chapter 1).

The Bad Apples: Has Anybody Committed Fraud in This Asset Class?

Unfortunately, yes. Let's look at one example. In September 2020, the SEC charged two executives from a San Francisco-based real estate investment firm with orchestrating a Ponzi scheme aimed at embezzling millions of dollars from hundreds of investors. The SEC alleged that a substantial portion of the money raised was misused for the executives' own personal expenses, including vacation homes and a failed development deal.

It was a classic Ponzi scheme: When the performance of the portfolio began to decline, the operators began to use new investor money to pay existing investors until the deal ran out of funds and collapsed—but not before they drained a large portion of the capital themselves. In the end, one of the executives passed away prior to being charged, and the other plead guilty to the charges, although the case is still pending.

What Are the Lessons to Be Learned?

When considering any deal in this space, learn about the operator's past mistakes, how upfront they were about their worst deals, and what they did when the deal went bad. Every operator has a failure story—if they say otherwise, run! As an investor, you should be able to accept an investment stopping distributions or a loss of capital because of a deal not performing as well as planned—as long as that was part of the original business plan and wasn't done behind closed doors. I have been in many deals where this has happened. While it's not the greatest feeling, it at least tells me that the operator is honest, and most of the time I find that there is a plan in place to restart the distributions.

What's not okay is when the operator takes sketchy steps that risk the collective investor capital by mixing new investor capital with fictional investment returns. As a rule, when someone invests in a fund, only the returns from the investments should be returned to them—nothing else unless it's clearly marked as a return of principal. This underscores why analyzing a fund's track record is critical. In our previous example, the Income Fund 7 and Growth Fund 4 titles indicated that six previous funds existed on the income side, with three previous funds on the growth side. This means that nine total previous funds exited without issues. That kind of track record goes a long way in establishing the trust of investors. Also, keep in mind that having multiple funds in this manner indicates that it is a closed-end fund, which only remains open for a set time period and a set raise. This is the opposite of an open-end fund, which as its name implies, can remain open indefinitely, at the discretion of the manager. Closed-end funds tend to eliminate possible Ponzi schemes because new capital can't be brought in to pay existing investors once the fund is closed. For this reason, you may want to avoid open-end funds as a new investor.

When considering any multi-asset fund, make sure that you understand the type of fund and the individual assets it includes before deciding whether it is right for you. And, as always, remember to diversify your portfolio and network with other individuals who have invested in the same or similar spaces.

The Pros and Cons of Investing in Multi-Asset Funds

PROS

- Instant diversification across asset classes, types, geographies, and time
- Operators usually have a long track record and deep client base that allows for better terms in individual projects
- Cash flow is not tied to one project

CONS

- You are investing based on the vision of the fund operator
- Limited supply of real estate-focused funds compared to single asset deals
- High minimum investments
- Due diligence involves more moving parts than a single deal or asset class
- Compensation structure can get complicated with fund fees, project fees, and profit splits

---

ASK THE EXPERTS: Q&A With Paul Moore

Disclaimer: This Q&A is provided for informational purposes only. You should seek your own advice from professional advisors, including lawyers, financial advisors, and accountants, regarding the legal, tax, and financial implications of any investment you contemplate.

Paul Moore is the founder and managing partner of Wellings Capital, a real estate private equity firm that manages several recession-resistant funds that give accredited investors access to a diversified portfolio, including different asset types, geographies, operators, properties, and strategies. With 20-plus years of experience in real estate investing, Paul has completed over 85 real estate investments and exits, appeared on HGTV's House Hunters, *rehabbed and managed dozens of rental properties, and developed a subdivision. After completing three successful real estate developments, including assisting with the development of a Hyatt hotel and a very successful multi-family project, Paul narrowed his focus to commercial real estate.*

When did you start investing?

I invested in a single commercial deal in 1999, then I started flipping houses in 2000. After doing dozens of homes, I began flipping waterfront lots. Then, I did new home construction and eventually got into multi-family by co-owning and operating two multi-family facilities in North Dakota starting in 2011.

How were you introduced to multi-asset funds?

I got a petroleum engineering degree in the '80s. When the North Dakota oil rush started around 2010, my business partner and I invested in an oil and gas deal that did not turn out so well. While there, we noticed that there were thousands of job openings and virtually no place for oil and gas workers to stay. There were "man camps," and RVs, and a lot of people sleeping in their pickup trucks. Some people were living doubled up in terrible circumstances, but they were making a lot of money. My business partner and I were both in real estate, so we bought 76 acres and quickly developed a multi-family facility to house oil workers. Then, we did another one next door. We operated both of them for a number of years and sold when oil prices were above $100 per barrel.

I then signed up for an expensive coaching program for multi-family, where I learned a lot about Class B value-add apartment projects. I even wrote a book called The Perfect Investment. I told my wife I would be staying in this lane for the rest of my career. After banging our heads against the wall for years looking for deals that made sense, we realized that multi-family was largely overheated.

We decided to expand into self-storage and later into mobile home parks. We found that there are a lot of mom-and-pop opportunities in self-storage and mobile home parks, which is something we had not seen in multi-family for years. We also noticed that a few operators were doing remarkably well—far better than the average. Since we had a few hundred potential investors waiting to give us money, we decided the best path would be to become a due diligence partner for these investors. We began researching the best operators and the best deals, and then investing in some of them. Later, we decided to set up a fund, and we are now in the process of finishing out our third one. These funds give investors access to carefully selected operators. We continue to research new operators, and our investors are benefiting by partnering with us.

What is the biggest negative you discovered?

The barriers to entry in commercial real estate: You need experience, a team, a lot of cash, and a high net worth, and you have to compete with a lot of other experienced operators to find deals. As in the residential market, the best deals are found off-market directly from the owners. When we discovered the wonderful aspects of investing in self-storage and mobile home parks, we realized that we did not have the track record, the experienced team, or the acquisition pipeline to be a top operator. But we had well over 100 investors waiting to invest, so we had a difficult decision to make. We had to decide if we wanted to become an operator or a due diligence partner for operators looking to invest in these asset classes. Furthermore, we saw a great benefit in diversifying one investor's funds across a lot of different assets, so at that point, we decided to launch a diversified fund.

What is your most memorable experience in this asset class?

Well, I've certainly had a lot of wonderful ups and painful downs during my decades investing in real estate. I hosted a podcast called How to Lose Money for four years, and we interviewed over 230 successful entrepreneurs, investors, and managers on their painful losses on the way to the top. Mine included!

So, I have to say it's been refreshing these last several years managing our Wellings recession-resistant funds that invest in self-storage and mobile home parks. So far, we've had very few disappointments and lots of great news. One of my happiest memories came in late 2020. In January 2020, we visited a Louisville mobile home park with 311 pads as part of due diligence. Our operating partner acquired it in February 2020 for $7.1 million, which consisted approximately half debt and half equity. A week later, he was offered $9.5 million, which he turned down. He said he thought it would be worth $12–$13 million within a few years once they did their magic. I was surprised he turned down such a great offer, but it was a wonderful move on his part, as it would turn out. There were three major arenas for improvement at this park. The owner had not been to the park for at least five years. She lived three states away, and her husband had passed away. Though it was run well, there were some deficiencies. First, it had 50 vacant lots. Second, the utilities were being paid by the owners. Third, the rents were 25%–35% below market. Our operating partner raised rents a little and passed all of the utilities back to the tenants, as is customary. This dramatically increased the value of the park, and he was starting a program to place up to 50 mobile homes on the vacant lots. He got an offer in August 2020 that he couldn't refuse, and he closed on the park to a buyer who paid $15 million in December. That is a 347% IRR at the project level and a 3.4 multiple on invested capital. This was a wonderful win, and even the buyer is getting a great park with the opportunity to fill in the vacant spaces, which will be a win for his investors over time.

What is a common misconception about multi-asset funds?

The most common misconception about self-storage is that it's a really easy business to run. People assume that after running apartment buildings or even single-family rentals and dealing with all the toilets, tenants, and trash that a self-storage facility must be easy. And it is easy to run a mediocre facility, but it is actually quite challenging to run a world-class facility. This is where the secret sauce is in this business: taking a mom-and-pop facility and upgrading it to a great facility.

Mom-and-pop operators don't have the desire or knowledge or resources to upgrade their assets. As a result, there are many *opportunities to add value. This is another misconception in self-storage: People don't believe there is value to add. Apartments have paint, wallpaper, counters, lighting, cabinets, and more that can be upgraded. What value-adds are available at a self-storage facility? I laughed when I first heard about this because I pictured four pieces of sheet metal, rivets, a door, and a floor, and wondered how you could improve upon that. But there are many value-adds in self-storage, including adding truck rentals, selling insurance, selling showroom items . . . like lock boxes, tape, and scissors, expanding the rentable area. Many mediocre self-storage facilities have doubled in value under new ownership, and that is the type of facility we love to invest in.*

Mobile home parks have a reputation for being slums, and investors have long turned their nose up at investing in these assets. Of course, this is a benefit for us now, as the world has awakened to this asset class and is now rushing in.

What is the most important thing an investor should know when considering a multi-asset fund?

In investing, it is critical to be an obsessive expert in your niche. That's why Warren Buffett, the greatest investor in the world, spends about six to eight hours reading almost daily. He is truly an expert, and we would all do well to follow him. If you think you can hold down a good-paying full-time job and do real estate investing on the side, you are probably going to fail. You will be competing against people who are obsessed with real estate and can probably get the best deals and make the best profits.

Most investors would be better off to invest passively and pay a professional a few percentage points to do all of the heavy lifting. In fact, if you find one of the best of the best professionals, you will probably make far more profit, and your effort will consist of going to the mailbox to pick up your checks every month. Passive investing is the best plan for most investors. Even Buffett does it this way. Think about it. He owns Dairy Queen, Geico, and many other companies, but he doesn't make ice cream, and he doesn't write insurance policies. Buffett relies on experts to do the heavy lifting, and he provides equity and guidance. We would all be wise to consider this option.

You also need to be extremely diligent in your review of the operators/syndicators/sponsors. You need to spend a lot of time getting to know them and doing deep background checks, criminal checks, reference checks, meeting them in person at their office, getting to know their team, looking at their track record, etc. You need to understand their debt and their projections. You need to hear what went wrong in the past and how they dealt with it. You need to understand their worst deal and their best deal, and why they think the current deal is a good one. Regardless of how much you like them, you need to take a cold, hard look at their numbers and also ask yourself if you have a great gut feeling about them. Left brain and right brain should both align here, or don't invest.

What is your professional background, and how did it affect your investing career?

After graduating with a BS in engineering and an MBA from Ohio State University, I worked at Ford Motor Company in Detroit for almost five years. Then I started a staffing firm with a partner, so I had the engineering history, the business side, and an entrepreneurial background. After getting involved with real estate, I also had an internet marketing firm for real estate leads. Along the way, I actually worked briefly with a cost segregation firm on commission, and that was very helpful for me. All of this helped me a lot when I got involved in commercial real estate in 2011. I am very grateful for even the wrong turns I took along the way. And there were many, believe me!

What information sources have been the most influential for you?

Personally, I have been deeply helped by the writings of psychologist Larry Crabb. His work on explaining the human condition and how to change has been very valuable to me.

Professionally, the concepts from The One Thing by Gary Keller and Jay Papasan have been very valuable because I have been a perpetual shiny object chaser. This has helped me focus on a daily, weekly, and long-term basis. The best references I've found on multi-asset funds include Brian Burke's book, The Hands-Off Investor. I've also really enjoyed the concepts Warren Buffett shares in his biography, The Snowball, and his annual meetings and letters. Buffett's hero and mentor Benjamin Graham has a few great books on investing, and his friend Howard Marks wrote the book Mastering the Market Cycle: Getting the Odds on Your Side.

There are many podcasts that have influenced me, including those from BiggerPockets and Hunter Thompson, and Richard C. Wilson's Family Office Club.

Who that you personally know do you most respect in business, and why?

I really respect Brian Burke, who is also featured in this book. There are a lot of great syndicators out there, but Brian has done an exceptional job in saying no a lot—which I've learned to love—and to creatively solve the problem of finding great deals in a seriously overheated multi-family market.

I also really admire Matt Ricciardella from Crystal View Capital. He has done a fantastic job in combing the nation to find the very best value-add opportunities in the mobile home park and self-storage space. He does more than just value add; he is an intrinsic value extractor. What I mean by that is that he can see potential in an asset in ways that most people would miss. This allows him to pay a very fair price to the seller, but still make fantastic returns for his company and his investors.

You are at a holiday party and asked what you do for a living. What do you say?

My company has created a diversified fund that offers investors an easy on ramp to access a pool of carefully vetted commercial operators in commercial real estate that provide outsized income and growth with limited downside risk.

What is the best piece of investing advice that you've ever received?

Paul Samuelson, the first U.S. economist to win the Nobel Peace Prize, said that investing should be boring. Specifically, he said,

"Investing should be like watching paint dry or watching grass grow. If you want excitement, take $800 and go to Las Vegas." The point of that is that there is a difference between investing and speculating, which is a major Warren Buffett tenet. Investing is when your principal is generally safe, and you have a chance to make a return. Speculating is when your principal is not at all safe, and you have a chance to make a return. Speculators may be more famous, but investors usually win in the long run.

What's your greatest alternative investment failure, and what would you do differently?

My greatest failures have almost always been when investing outside what I know. For example, after having tremendous success in building and operating the multi-family in North Dakota, we decided to expand into wireless internet in the same region. We had a team of people who knew how to do it in Tennessee, but not in the bitter tundra up there. We spent years and hundreds of thousands of dollars to get it profitable, but it never got there. It was a huge distraction, a waste of money, and an embarrassment for the small group of investors we pulled together. I've had several occasions like this where I got off my main game and lost time or money. I hope to never do it again.

In five years, do you still see yourself investing in this niche?

I absolutely believe I will still be investing in mobile home parks and self-storage. Hopefully, I'll be doing some multi-family again. I always have my eye out for additional recession-resistant assets. I know there will come a day when self-storage and mobile home parks are not as fragmented as they are today, but while the sun is shining, we're going to make as much hay as possible in these amazing niches!

ASK THE EXPERTS: Q&A With Mark Cira

Disclaimer: This Q&A is provided for informational purposes only. You should seek your own advice from professional advisors, including lawyers, financial advisors, and accountants, regarding the legal, tax, and financial implications of any investment you contemplate.

Mark Cira and his wife are co-founders of Cira Capital Group, a firm that helps other busy professionals invest in private real estate without having to become an expert themselves. They focus on helping others diversify their portfolios, both away from the stock market and within real estate. In the near-term, they plan to offer a diversified fund that will provide maximum diversification with minimal effort from investors. In addition, they are partners in the founding of Upward Communities, a company focused on providing safe, clean, attractive, and affordable manufactured housing communities.

When did you start investing?

My wife first introduced me to real estate in 2007 through her family's general contracting business in Chicago. We purchased our first piece of land shortly after getting married and began building single-family homes and condos in 2012. A few years later, we decided to pursue additional ways to invest through syndicated private real estate. We invested with a few operators and started to discuss what we were doing with our friends and family. When they asked us to help them invest in real estate, we decided to start Cira Capital Group.

How were you introduced to multi-asset funds?

I was introduced to funds through lots of research into the options for private real estate investing, reading, and attending a lot of conferences. I've never felt adequately diversified with my real estate investing, and that has led me to start investing more in funds. It also sparked an interest in starting my own fund that focuses on diversification.

What is the biggest negative you discovered?

Funds and their legal structure provide limited transparency to financial performance and asset operations. In addition, fees can be opaque, and liquidity is generally unavailable.

That being said, unless you're ultra-wealthy, I don't see a good alternative for investing in real estate except through funds. It's nearly impossible to be truly diversified in private real estate without at least $1 million dedicated to individual deals and/or funds. And, contrary to many real estate investors, I still believe that you should maintain some of your net worth in equities. I believe a balanced portfolio would allocate no more than about 25–35% to real estate, with the remainder in equities, bonds, cash, and a small amount in speculative alternatives, such as cryptocurrencies, precious metals, and start-up or angel funds. So, if you were to invest in individual real estate deals at $25,000 per deal, it would take a total portfolio of $2–$3 million (including non-real estate assets) to have a truly balanced portfolio. Most people don't have that kind of portfolio, so the only way to reach diversification in real estate is to invest in multiple funds in smaller increments.

What is your most memorable experience in this asset class?

I remember when the lightbulb went off for me related to real estate. When we sold our first two development homes, I had a pile of cash that I had to figure out what to do with next. That was memorable. Then, the bulb got a lot brighter a few years later at the first Intelligent Investors Real Estate Conference. I was listening to Jeremy Roll and other seasoned professionals talk about how they had invested in real estate to generate income and wealth, which allowed them to break out of the corporate world. I was sold.

What is a common misconception about multi-asset funds?

It's not worth the fees, or there's too much fee duplication. I think if you invest with the right operators, you're paying for expertise, and that expertise—coupled with the diversification you achieve— pays for itself in reduced risk. Similar to everything from dining out to going to the doctor, you utilize experts every day to do things or provide services that you cannot do yourself. Using funds managed by experts is no different.

What is the most important thing an investor should know when considering an investment a multi-asset fund?

Like every investment in private real estate, the operator's track record is the most important. Talk to other investors, ask what their *experience has been and what feedback they have. Be very skeptical of investing in new operators with no track record.*

I also believe strongly in transparency. Ray Dalio preaches radical transparency in his businesses. I have seen time and time again the profits and perils of sharing or hiding information. It rarely helps to hoard information. Bad news never gets better, and good news only gets stale. So make sure operators are providing timely information and being open and honest with their progress and results.

What is your professional background, and how did it affect your investing career?

I have a BS in accounting from Iowa State University and am a registered CPA in Illinois. I started my career as a consultant in the legal industry, providing advice on mega project construction management issues, dispute mediations, and claims and lawsuits. All of these have contributed to my ability to review investment materials, pro formas, etc., and evaluate operators and their offerings. I have also worked for a variety of consulting and accounting firms over nearly 20 years and continue to apply that knowledge to the security, energy, and construction industries.

What information sources have been the most influential for you?

My favorite book on real estate investing is Investing in Real Estate Private Equity: An Insider's Guide to Real Estate Partnerships, Funds, Joint Ventures & Crowdfunding. *It covers the fundamentals for investing in all types of real estate private equity. It also touches on the topic of diversification and how to build a balanced portfolio that does not expose you to exceptional risks in any one area.*

Joe Fairless's podcast and books are great starter materials, while Hunter Thompson's podcast and book are great for advanced investors. I also read and listen to The Economist, Marketplace, EconTalk *(Russ Roberts),* Against the Rules *(Michael Lewis),* People I (Mostly) Admire, *and* Freakonomics.

Who that you personally know do you most respect in business, and why?

Jeremy Roll—he set a goal in 2002 to exit corporate America and become a full time "passive" investor, and he achieved it five years later. He's been a full-time passive investor for about 20 years and has a tremendous wealth of information. I appreciate his dedication to sharing his deep knowledge to educate others and help them make good decisions with their investments.

You are at a holiday party and asked what you do for a living. What do you say?

This is a hard question to answer for me because I have many lines of business. I usually say I am the CFO of a consulting firm and passive real estate aficionado.

What is the best piece of investing advice that you've ever received?

Real estate investing is not a get-rich-quick scheme. It's a get-rich-slow business. It takes discipline and patience to start accumulating wealth that can turn a snowflake into a glacier.

Also, "passive income" doesn't really exist, and there are no free rides. You're either going to do the work yourself or pay someone else to do it in order to cultivate returns. Someone has to find, manage, operate, organize, and otherwise run the business of investing in real estate.

What's your greatest alternative investment failure, and what would you do differently?

When I first started investing, I got a little too excited and allocated far too much money to individual assets and operators. In retrospect, I believe that was a huge rookie mistake. Although the investments are performing well so far, it could have been detrimental to my real estate returns. That's what helped me form my thesis on diversification through funds.

In five years, do you still see yourself investing in this niche?

Yes, I think I will be investing even more heavily in this niche. It took me a few years to figure out what my preferred strategy was for investing in real estate. Now that I understand the options, strategies, and vehicles, I plan to focus on building a diversified real estate portfolio that will provide steady and predictable returns long into my retirement. Because most syndications and funds last five to ten years and have limited liquidity, there's only one option: start now!

TAKEAWAYS

- A great way to diversify if you understand the individual assets that make up the fund
- Most funds are open to accredited investors only
- Leverage your network for the best operators
- Minimum investment amount could be higher than typical syndications
- Make sure you choose a multi-asset fund type that fits your existing portfolio
- Choose a close-ended fund for your first investment in this space

10
ATM FUNDS

"Digital currencies have gained traction in the last couple of years, but cash in circulation has all but doubled in the last decade."
—Dave Zook, bestselling author and ATM industry expert

Automated Teller Machine (ATM) funds have one of the most unique business models out of any niche in this book. To illustrate, let's do a quick review. High-equity life insurance policies provide a slow and steady approach to building wealth. Life insurance settlements are a long-term diversification play banking on the one thing in life that's guaranteed: death. Apartment buildings are an investment on the favorable trend of renters over homeowners and usually provide a combination of appreciation and cash flow. But if you're looking for a pure cash flow investment, look no further. ATM funds are a cash flow play on steroids, thanks to the aggressive contractual rate of return to the investor.

Let's take a closer look at why this is so.

What Is the Asset?
An ATM is a machine that allows customers to complete a wide range of banking transactions, such as transfers, withdrawals, paying bills, and deposits without the assistance of a bank associate. ATMs usually operate 24/7/365, allowing customers to

bank whenever is convenient for them, even outside of traditional banking hours. In exchange for the convenience of using an ATM, the operator usually charges a set fee to the customer, except in the case where fees are waived as a member benefit to existing bank customers. The same courtesy is also sometimes extended by some smaller banks and credit unions with limited locations. According to Moneyrates.com, the average fee to withdraw cash from an out-of-network ATM in 2019 was $4.61.[31] These fees can add up to $240 per year for a customer that uses an out-of-network machine weekly. According to an FDIC survey, an estimated 5.4% or 7.1 million U.S. households were unbanked in 2019, meaning that they didn't hold a checking or savings account with a traditional banking institution. Even within the banked population, a staggering 19.5% of households preferred using the ATMS as their primary tool[32] for taking care of banking needs. This represents a large ATM customer pool for the foreseeable future.

An ATM machine may be owned by a bank, credit union, or private investment entity. Because ATMs are expensive and become technologically obsolete after only seven years, most larger retailers and even some financial institutions outsource to private entities that place ATM machines at their location and split the fees. While a private entity may be a private investor, the contracts that a single investor may procure are typically limited to a small

---

[31] Julia Kagan, "Automated teller machine (ATM)," Investopedia (January 28, 2021), https://www.investopedia.com/terms/a/atm.asp.

[32] "How America banks: Household use of banking and financial services," FDIC Survey (2019), https://www.fdic.gov/analysis/household-survey/.

convenience store or comparable outlet. Large corporate entities, like national pharmacy chains, contract with larger private equity funds that specialize in ATMs. As an investor, whether or not you invest in an ATM fund or individual machine, your due diligence will vary based on how the investment is structured. For the purposes of this book, we will focus on the ATM fund model.

Private equity funds pool their investors' money to buy a batch of new ATMs, and the fund operator contract breaks out the total return to those investors into equal months payments for seven years. During this period, the operator is entitled to any profit above the contracted rate. At the end of the contract, the investor may receive a token amount of their original principal back, but in reality, they should not expect this. The investment is unique because it provides such a strong influx of cash during its investment life. For this reason, ATM funds are a great complement to investments that don't provide cash flow right away.

ATMs are also on the cutting edge of gathering data on end users. Given the high volume of daily transactions they process, ATMs can glean an incredible amount of information that the operator can then sell or use for their own advertisement purposes. However, since this is very much a developing trend, it should not be modeled in any investor projections.

What Is the History of the Asset?

The first prototypes of the modern-day ATM were introduced in the 1960s in the United Kingdom.[33] Later that decade, early versions of the machines were introduced in Spain, Australia, Sweden, and the United States, but the technology at the time was highly error-prone and reliant on tokens with complicated pins.

As the technology improved over the next decade, ATMs became a powerful and more ubiquitous tool for growing retail banks and cash businesses, like restaurants, that operate after banking hours. Banks began viewing ATMs as an opportunity to better connect digitally with underbanked customers—those who have bank accounts but often turn elsewhere for financial transaction support. Unfortunately, they also saw them as an opportunity to cut their workforce and focus their smaller labor footprint on higher margin add-on services, like insurance, investments, and credit cards[34].

In the 1990s, two major technological advances changed the ATM industry: First, the dedicated telephone lines that ATMs were originally connected to were replaced by a digital version; and second, the Microsoft Windows® operating system was introduced. For the first time in the industry, troubleshooting could be performed remotely, and credit card clearance networks were integrated within the network for a faster response time. Both changes reaccelerated growth in the industry and created a need

---

[33] Bernardo Bátiz-Lazo, "A brief history of the ATM," *The Atlantic* (March 26, 2015), https://www.theatlantic.com/technology/archive/2015/03/a-brief-history-of-the-atm/388547/.

[34] Ibid.

for centralization of ATMs that were not associated with major banks. That need was filled by the emergence of the independent ATM deployer (IAD), an entity that owns and manages ATMs, handling everything from location selection to installation, maintenance and repairs, cash management, processing, and security oversight.

Some predicted that the last decade would be the beginning of the end for ATMs, as new digital technologies emerged that allowed individuals to exchange cash and make payments virtually. However, ATM usage and cash circulation are still trending upward and continue to play a critical role for the underbanked population around the world. Many argue that a tipping point needs to be reached before digital currencies will completely replace the functionality of ATMs, but there is an opposing opinion that supports the ability of ATMs to coexist alongside digital currencies with the addition of future-focused functionality enhancements.

What Are the Current Regulations on Buying and Selling the Asset?

While the regulations for an investor in individual ATMs and an investor in ATM funds are completely different, ATM funds should be the focus for passive investors, at least when starting out. Keep in mind that these funds are usually 506(c) Regulation D offerings, which require proof of investor accreditation when subscribing to the fund.

What Is the Market for the Asset?

As in most syndications, this asset is illiquid. The business model that I've encountered offers a high return of capital over the first few years of the contract, and there is no incentive to sell after that point because none of your original investment is left in the deal.

The Bad Apples: Has Anybody Committed Fraud in This Asset Class?

ATM funds deal with a higher volume of cash transactions that lend themselves to disreputable operators looking to take advantage of investors; therefore, the ATM fund industry has a history of more Ponzi schemes compared to other alternative assets.

In one case in October 2009, the Southern District of New York indicted two ATM operators for an $80 million Ponzi scheme. The investors in the case weren't purchasing ATM machines according to the terms of the deal. In fact, out of the 4,000 ATMs that were supposed to be in the fund, only 400 were actually in use and contributing to the fund's revenue; the rest of the money was coming from new investors to pay old investors. It's important to note that it's not the ATM machine that stole the investors' money. It was two bad operators. But sadly, cases like this give the entire industry a black mark.

In light of these vexing issues, I was particularly fortunate when Jeremy Roll, a highly regarded investor with more than a decade of ATM investing experience, agreed to participate in this chapter. Jeremy is the co-founder of For Investors by Investors (FIBI), a non-profit organization created to facilitate the networking of investors, and he has a very loyal following of over 1,500 passive investors. Those who know Jeremy personally know that his ability to perform due diligence is second to no other investor. I once spoke to an operator, and the conversation drifted toward Jeremy. The word the operator used to describe Jeremy's due diligence was "painful."

I never forget the moment I heard that term used; I immediately felt that should be a gold standard in our industry.

To be fair, an operator may not be willing to go through a "painful" due diligence process just for a minimum investment from a single investor, but somewhere in the middle of what Jeremy calls "proper due diligence" and just taking the operator's word lies a happy medium (hopefully skewed toward Jeremy's approach).

Jeremy would be the first to admit that proper due diligence requires an extensive knowledge of the asset class. If you are at the stage where you are still learning basic industry jargon, you should probably avoid attempts at performing a painful due diligence yourself, and instead focus your energy on networking with other investors and learning the asset class better. Increase the "pain" in proportion to your confidence that you know what you're talking about.

In Jeremy's career, he successfully identified three potential Ponzi schemes. In hindsight, they were very easy to spot, but doing so preemptively on three different occasions with three different operators is how you earn a stellar reputation like Jeremy's. Let's take a look at his due diligence workflow:

1) Make sure a prospective operator provides all of the proper investment documents at the time of the investor presentation. These include the offering (Private Placement Memorandum) and the operating agreement. It's a huge red flag if the operator says anything along the lines of, "Our attorney is working on it, and we will get it over to you if you commit."

2) Do a background check on all of the operators involved in a deal. Jeremy once found an operator that was convicted of credit card terminal fraud only to later try his hand at ATMs. You can imagine the result.

3) Verify the physical locations and functionality of the existing ATMs. Anybody can do this; it just takes work.

4) Perform a terminal log in to see the real-time ATM portfolio and its live transactions. This requires the operator to provide a look behind the scenes of their operations, and it can be a tough sell if you're a small investor.

5) Ensure that the operators have proper IAD/ISO certification indicating that they are audited every one to two years by a third-party financial institution. The most important part of this step is ensuring that the operators are the ones complying with the audit directly, rather than being paired with someone else who is certified. No certification, no investment—period!

6) Perform a status check with a processing company, such as VISA. In conjunction with your findings in Step 3, you should be able to see that each specific ATM is listed on the processing company's portal.

Sounds pretty grueling, right? The good news is that if you find an operator that passes all six steps on this due diligence checklist, you will have taken a significant step toward protecting yourself. Circling back to the Ponzi scheme mentioned in the earlier example, the operators wouldn't have passed Step 3 if the investor had obtained a list of the ATMs and randomly selected a few to physically visit. Think of the odds: If the investor only visited one random ATM on the list, there is only a 10% chance that they would have found that unit there in working order and been able to match it to the transaction log (Step 4). Now if that same investor visited a second ATM machine, the chances of finding a properly placed and operating machine would go down to 1%. You can see what would happen if this investor chose ten random machines for inspection.

What Are the Lessons to Be Learned?
While most alternative investments—especially those related to real estate—are tax friendly, they require extensive tax planning in order to be executed properly. Investing in ATMs is probably the exception. While these funds are also very tax friendly, they require only minimal tax planning. Because the life expectancy of an ATM is only five to ten years, investors receive a substantial depreciation write-off during many of the years of their investment. At the end of the investment, because the investor receives almost nothing back, their tax liability is marginalized. Remember to consult with a tax professional to see how ATM funds would work within your specific portfolio.

The Pros and Cons of Investing in ATM Funds
PROS
- Massive cash flow
- Backed by a contract and location
- High depreciation creates favorable tax treatment
- Provides access to cash for underbanked and unbanked demographics
- New technology facilitates new revenue streams related to data collection and advertisements
- Strategically placed ATMs fared well during the COVID-19 pandemic

CONS
- Concerns about technological obsolescence
- Targeting consumers in low-income communities can be viewed as predatory
- High prevalence of Ponzi schemes
- Business model can sometimes be murky

ASK THE EXPERTS: Q&A With Dave Zook

Disclaimer: This Q&A is provided for informational purposes only. You should seek your own advice from professional advisors, including lawyers, financial advisors, and accountants, regarding the legal, tax, and financial implications of any investment you contemplate.

Dave Zook is a successful business owner and experienced real estate investor active in multi-family apartments, self-storage, ATMs, and commodity and energy-related projects. Since 2010, Dave has acquired more than $200 million worth of real estate. Together with his business partner, Dave is a renowned and trusted professional resource in the ATM investment market, where he and his partners are heavily invested personally and where they have deployed more than $200 million of investor capital. As a #1 best-selling author and sought-after speaker, Dave has shared his knowledge at the International Business Conference, The Jason Hartman Real Estate mastermind, The Wealth Formula *Podcast, and* The Real Estate Guys Radio Show. *Dave is also a faculty member and presenter at The Secrets of Successful Syndication Seminar. Dave lives with his wife Susan and their four children in Lancaster County, PA.*

When did you start investing?

I started investing when I was 17 years old. I bought a truck and started pulling prefabricated modular buildings on nights and weekends to make extra cash. It was part of my family's business, so it was easy to get into. As soon as I got my license, I got a truck. I feel that I was born an entrepreneur. Although I worked a full-time schedule at my family's modular construction business, I saw the benefits of creating that additional income during my off hours.

How were you introduced to ATM funds?

Bill Poole, who is a good friend of mine who later joined my advisor team, got involved in the ATM industry. It was through his network that I was introduced to the space back in 2011. I started off as a passive investor for a couple of years. During this period, I was investing heavily in multi-family apartment buildings and syndicating my own deals. At one point, the operators of the ATM deal that I invested in passively reached out to partner with them. In 2016, I joined their team.

Since I started, I have been involved with only one operator—first, as a passive investor and then as an operating partner.

What is the biggest negative you discovered?

In 2011, it was rumored that there was a new wave of digital technology being released, and that cash circulation would be decreasing once these currencies gained ubiquity. The operating team that I invested in walked me through their thesis on why that wouldn't be the case and also highlighted how the target user was part of the population called the unbanked. Those digital accounts would have to be linked to actual bank accounts, which they didn't have. I trusted their expertise and felt that the positives outweighed the one negative that I could find. I went through with the investment and was rewarded for trusting the operating team. The digital currencies have gained traction in the last couple of years, but the cash circulation has increased over the last decade—and the unbanked demographic has remained steady.

What is your most memorable experience in this asset class?

During the Baltimore riots, two of our ATMs were stolen and taken to a machine shop. Unfortunately for the robbers, we had upgraded our vaults to bank-grade vaults. Even with industrial torches, they could not access the contents of the safe, and we later recovered the ATMs fully intact. Those were the only two ATMs that were ever vandalized. Besides that incident and what you see in movies, it's actually been pretty boring—which is the way I like my investments.

What is a common misconception about ATM funds?

The general rule is that if you have enough money to invest in an ATM, you are probably not an ATM user. Most investors are credit card users, so they assume that since they don't use the ATM that no one uses the ATM.

What is the most important thing an investor should know when considering an ATM fund?

The classic phrase "location, location, location" comes to mind right away. Investing in an ATM is similar to any real estate play. It's similar to how you would try to add value by developing ten acres of land for its best use. When you're investing in ATMs, you're taking real estate located on a 3-foot by 3-foot parcel and extracting the maximum value out of it.

A great location doesn't mean just volume of people. You can have a high-traffic location, but if it's in a wealthy location, you won't have any customers. There's a reason why there aren't many ATM machines in Louis Vuitton stores. You have to be located in the right area that mainly services ATM users: low-income areas with EBT (Electronic Benefit Transfer) users and other underbanked populations.

What is your professional background, and how did it affect your investing career?

I grew up in my family's manufacturing business. I worked there and my side hustle until I was 22 years old. I got to perform so many different tasks in the business that I felt it gave me a great overall background to try other businesses. After I left the family business, I tried a variety of different things that didn't work. Eventually, some things began to click, and I stuck to those and then began leveraging what did work and scaled up from there.

What information sources have been the most influential for you?

Business book: Rich Dad Poor Dad *by Robert Kiyosaki*
Podcast: The Real Estate Guys
Personal book: The Compound Effect *by Darren Hardy*

Who that you personally know do you most respect in business, and why?

One that stands out is a local business in my area, Shady Maple restaurant in Lancaster, PA. It has a great reputation and is second-generation owned. They take pride in what they do. What I admire most is the culture that was built by the founders, Marvin and Miriam Weaver, and is carried on by the next generation, Linford and Phil Weaver.

You are at a holiday party and asked what you do for a living. What do you say?

I put investment packages together for investors and help them create additional income streams and reduce their tax liability. In short, I am a tax and financial strategist.

What is the best piece of investment advice that you've ever received?

Invest in yourself first. Then, once you locate and like the asset class, invest more time and energy into the team than into the actual asset. Eventually, the ATM asset class grew on me, but what sold me on the deal was the operating team's great track record, business background, and the respect they had from other investors whom I trusted.

What's your greatest alternative investment failure, and what would you do differently?

I invested in the wrong team in the multi-family space. What I would do differently is be more careful on who I teamed up with.

In five years, do you still see yourself investing in this niche?

It depends on what's going on around us. If in five years, the next seven years look strong, then sure, but I wouldn't be able to tell today. My team and I evaluate the ATM environment on a daily and weekly basis.

ASK THE EXPERTS: Q&A With Jeremy Roll

Disclaimer: This Q&A is provided for informational purposes only. You should seek your own advice from professional advisors, including lawyers, financial advisors, and accountants, regarding the legal, tax, and financial implications of any investment you contemplate.

Jeremy Roll started investing in real estate and businesses in 2002, leaving the corporate world in 2007 to become a full-time passive cash flow investor. He is currently an investor in more than 60 opportunities across more than $1 billion worth of real estate and business assets. As founder and president of Roll Investment Group, Jeremy manages a group of over 1,500 investors who seek passive/managed cash flowing investments in real estate and businesses. Jeremy is also the co-founder of For Investors By Investors (FIBI), a non-profit organization that facilitates networking and learning among real estate investors in a strict no sales pitch environment. FIBI is now the largest group of public real estate investor meetings in California with over 30,000 members. Jeremy, who holds an MBA from The Wharton School, is a licensed California real estate broker (for investing purposes only) and an advisor for Realty Mogul, the largest real estate crowdfunding website in the U.S. He welcomes opportunities to network with and help other investors, and to discuss real estate or business investments of any size.

When did you start investing?

I started investing in passive alternative opportunities in real estate and businesses back in 2002. I was looking for more predictability and less volatility after the dot-com crash. So my initial focus was on more predictable, lower-risk cash flowing opportunities, and it remains the same today.

How were you introduced to ATM funds?

In 2008, I met an ATM operator in Los Angeles during the first ever "For Investors by Investors" networking event that I was launching. The turnout was very small, and the fact that a successful ATM operator was one of the attendees was very fortuitous. I am a believer that you never know who you will run into at any networking event. My relationship with that operator has now lasted over 13 years and continues on today.

What is the biggest negative you discovered?

This is a well-known asset class for Ponzi schemes because you're typically investing in a large pool of assets, which makes it hard to track. It also has very high projected returns relative to other asset classes, which makes it easier for unscrupulous operators to attract new investors.

The second biggest downside is that many investors don't believe that ATMs will be around in ten-plus years because of digital alternatives and the possibility that cash will be used less in the coming years (even though current data shows that, unlike what most people would expect, the use of cash continues to increase annually).

Ultimately, I did end up investing in the space because it came down to who you are making a bet on. In this particular situation, I felt confident that the operator that I met at the For Investors By Investors networking event was not running a Ponzi scheme. That confidence came from getting to know the operator for an extended period of time and performing background checks and visiting the actual ATMs in person to verify their existence and transaction levels. I also thought the timing was perfect since this operator was transitioning into an expansion mode after self-financing their own portfolio of 25 ATMs. For the first time, they were looking for outside investors, which allowed me to secure fair but favorable terms and to break even after only three years. The quick break even took considerable risk off the table for me. I *started by putting my toe in the water, and as I became more comfortable with the operator and the industry, I began to scale my ATM investments.*

It's important to note that the original operator I invested in wasn't a fund, and I was able to invest in individual machines. By doing so, I was provided log-in information to see the ATM transactions in real time from one of the largest processing companies in the U.S. While the risk didn't drop to zero, I felt good enough to get started.

In terms of the digital alternative argument for not investing, I still see opportunities in the space because I believe the adoption levels in the "underbanked" communities to be very slow, and they likely won't upend the need for cash for some time. But this concern is something I evaluate on a yearly basis.

What is your most memorable experience in this asset class?

The most memorable positive experience was a triple-digit annual return from an ATM placed in a medical marijuana retailer several years ago.

The most memorable negative experience came from a different medical marijuana store that was raided by the FBI. The ATM was confiscated, including the cash inside, for over a year until the case was resolved. Part of my negotiated terms with this specific operator allowed me to transfer my cash flow obligation to another ATM, so that negative experience didn't impact me financially (although it clearly impacted the operator, as the FBI confiscated both the ATM machine and the operator's cash inside that machine). This is a good example of how something can go wrong with this asset.

The worst ATM investing story I have is due to the COVID-19 pandemic. One of my operators had a focus on smaller retailers, like corner stores, saloons, and other smaller establishments, which were deemed unessential and were forced to close either temporarily or permanently. I wasn't able to transfer my cash flow during this period, but I was able to negotiate a buyout for my existing locations with my ATM operator, who thankfully gave me a more-than-fair deal.

Ironically, I invested in a second operator who had very few challenges during the pandemic because their ATMs were placed in locations that were deemed essential, like Walgreens and CVS. They actually saw an uptick in business during COVID, likely because many other ATMs were inaccessible in other retail locations that were closed.

It was an interesting dynamic to see the difference in how the pandemic affected different operators in the same space.

What is a common misconception about ATM funds?

Accredited investors may have a hard time relating to the end user of an ATM transaction. The investor needs to understand where the revenue is coming from, which is typically the non-banked and underbanked, instead of making a general assumption that people will use less cash in the future, as that might not be true of this particular segment of consumers.

For example, I have never used an ATM where I had to pay the transaction fee because I hated the concept of it. But there are a lot of people out there that do. In many cases, banks and credit unions cover those fees for their account holders. It's important for the investor to make that distinction even if it's not their personal experience (i.e., investors have to separate their subjective perspective from the objective data/reality).

One more misconception is that digital technology has reduced the cash in circulation. What's crazy is that the use of cash actually increased during the last few years when you look at the data. It's honestly hard for me to believe due to my own perception, but that's what the data shows. It's important not to make assumptions but look at the data to see if the ATM business model would be supported by future transactions. Even if a disruptor of cash does emerge in the future (from current companies or new alternatives), there would need to be an industry standard in the digital currency space. Those rules and the regulation that comes with it typically takes years to finalize, and then it typically takes years afterward for true mass adoption to occur. So I think it's unlikely that there will be a huge disruption to ATM transaction volumes in the short term and at once, but time will tell.

What is the most important thing an investor should know when considering an ATM fund?

Look for signs that you may be investing in a Ponzi scheme. While I am not an investment advisor, I was able to pre-identify three future Ponzi schemes during my due diligence. What became red flags to me in those deals were the following:

— Some did not have their investment documents (offering, ppm, investor summary) up to date or available. If they did have them, they wouldn't share them unless I was ready to move forward.

— In one case, I asked to visit the head office of the ATM company so I could meet them in person, look at their computer systems, and watch them log in to see the machines in their portfolio. Although their head office was supposedly only 30 minutes away from me in Los Angeles, they refused to let me meet with them. My intuition was right, and eight years later, that company turned out to be running one of the biggest Ponzi schemes in the history of Southern California.

— In another situation, I conducted a background check and saw that the operator was convicted of fraud in a similar industry (debit card transactions and hardware) and moved on to ATM machines once that was broken up. A different investor asked me to look into the operator, and after I discovered the history of fraud, I instructed them to spot check the locations they had already invested in to make sure all of the ATMs were actually in those locations. Sure enough, half of the ATMs didn't exist. The investor confronted the operator and received his investment back. If he waited much longer, who knows what would have happened? But if he would have performed a background check up front, he would have avoided what could have been a very big investment loss.

— Not being a registered independent ATM deployer (IAD). It's a big plus when you can invest with an IAD because they are sponsored, audited, and supervised by a financial institution (i.e., bank). I have never seen a Ponzi scheme in this space that involved an IAD because it involves a lot of unnecessary work for the operator to become one, and it's very difficult to cover up fraud when they're being regularly monitored by a bank. So the level of risk when investing with an IAD is clearly lower, but it's important to note that it's definitely not zero.

What is your professional background, and how did it affect your investing career?

I spent ten-plus years in the corporate world in marketing and finance positions (with both small and multiple Fortune 500 companies) before becoming a full-time passive cash flow investor. I also have an MBA from The Wharton School. My finance and MBA background definitely gave me an advantage when I started performing due diligence on opportunities early on (for example, I was very familiar with spreadsheets, financial analysis, etc.), and now that I have 19+ years of investing experience, I have been able to learn a lot from my experiences over time.

What information sources have been the most influential for you?

Two books I always recommend: Rich Dad Poor Dad and Cash Flow Quadrant by Robert Kiyosaki, in that order. On a personal level, I hardly ever read books, but I do read about two to three hours of business news a day to stay on top of the latest data and trends and help me continuously refine my investing strategy and focus. From a mindset perspective, I highly recommend watching or listening to Jim Rohm. I feel that his advice is timeless.

Who that you personally know do you most respect in business, and why?

One that comes to mind immediately is Mark Roberson. Like me, he has been investing full time for years and is careful with his due diligence. Mark has also started a robust community online to help other investors.

You are at a holiday party and asked what you do for a living. What do you say?

I am a full-time passive cash flow investor. If the answer is met with confusion (which it honestly often is, and which I can understand), I usually clarify that I am a real estate investor that focuses on cash flow. That typically allows people to more easily understand what I do.

What is the best piece of investing advice that you've ever received?

Watch for operators that oversubscribe the cash flow produced by one machine. An investor tends to stop their due diligence on ATMs once they verify that the machine physically exists. However, the operator may assign that same ATM machine not only to you, but to 20 other investors (which is fraudulent, but unfortunately can occur). One way to reduce this risk is to ask the operator for something in writing showing that you are the only investor assigned to that ATM's cash flow. Whether it's investing in ATMs or any other asset type, diversification is always critical, so diversifying across ATM operators will also help to reduce your risk.

247

What's your greatest alternative investment failure, and what would you do differently?

Not taking into account the fact that background players can become major players in the deal. I once invested in a real estate opportunity that involved a three-partner group. I was introduced to the two main partners. The third partner had an IT background, was focused on the back-end systems of the business, and was, therefore, not involved in the on-the-ground, day-to-day operations of the real estate. As a result, I focused my due diligence on the two key operating partners and felt comfortable with the deal. Shortly after I invested, there was a partner dispute, and the two operating partners who I had focused on resigned from the company, leaving the other partner in charge unexpectedly who I both didn't know well and who wasn't right the person to lead the operations and execution of a real estate business. I call this type of unlikely and unexpected event a 1% risk. To me, a 1% risk can materialize on the lower risk opportunities on which I focus when multiple dominoes fall in succession—similar to how a newer airplane needs multiple bad events to typically occur before it will crash due to the redundant systems and other safety measures that are in place. This is in contrast to an older plane where there's a lot of wear and tear and where perhaps only one domino needs to fall (i.e., cracks in the plane's fuselage that occur over long time periods) for the plane to crash. In the investing world, the "one domino" scenario is more common on higher risk opportunities like new ground-up real estate developments. There are fewer dominoes needed to fall for a bad outcome to occur due to the higher risk.

Going back to my example, the unlikely event that I never saw coming (the 1% risk) came to fruition. First, the two main operators *resigned. Then, the background operator took charge and proceeded to mismanage operations due to their lack of experience, instead of the more common solution of hiring a third-party property management company. In the end, I stepped in on behalf of investors, negotiated with the partner to hand over the properties to us to manage, hired a new property manager, stabilized the properties, and eventually sold them at roughly break even. A 0% return is typically a bad outcome for investors, but it was good in this situation given the challenges we experienced. It was a great lesson in terms of being sure to thoroughly vet even background partners and not just those who appear to be the key partners in an opportunity.*

When you invest in alternative assets, you always have to be mindful of the 1% risk. There are many different ways any investment can go bad, and even with the best due diligence the chance of fraud or an unlikely event to occur is always present, even if it's only 1%. That is why you always have to diversify across asset classes, geographies, and operators to help reduce some of the risks.

In five years, do you still see yourself investing in this niche?

I see myself still invested in the ATM business. I just wouldn't be able to say if I will be deploying new capital into ATMs at that time, as it will depend on how new uses of cash and technologies evolve over time, but I am quite confident I will still be invested in this asset class at that time. I would have to evaluate the actual cash in circulation and what new technology is available at that time to be able to tell you whether I would deploy more capital into this asset class at that time. A common break-even period for investors in this asset class is three to five years, and right now, I don't see a new technology in that horizon that would stop me from at least recouping my initial investment, so I am planning on deploying more capital in ATM opportunities in 2021. It's just too early to tell about 2026.

TAKEAWAYS

- Follow the "painful" due diligence checklist before investing
- Make sure you're comfortable with this asset class for at least the next five to seven years; if not, don't invest
- Fits well in a diversified portfolio that needs cash flow
- Potential significant tax benefits due to depreciation; consult an accountant
- Accredited investor status required to invest in a 506(c) Reg D ATM fund offering

---

11

TECH STARTUPS

"ARD does not invest in the ordinary sense. Rather, it creates by taking calculated risks in selected companies in whose growth it believes."
—Georges Doriot, Harvard Professor and President of American Research and Development Corporation, one of the first U.S. venture capital firms

Some common themes have emerged during the course of my networking with other investors. First, I've noticed that a disproportionate number of successful investors and operators come from an engineering background (with project managers and accountants both coming in a close second). I think their engineering mindset gives them the unique ability to look at an investment, break it down into smaller components, and then build it back in a way that makes sense to them. So what might appear risky, as a whole, to the average investor may actually appear safe to an engineer who's familiar with the smaller components of the deal.

The second theme is the topic of investing in start-up technology companies. It comes up over and over again during my networking calls. Admittedly, most investors who bring it up have worked in the tech space and therefore operate in a certain comfort zone when looking at such deals. I am definitely not one of them. Luckily,

Matt Canning, a Fortune 50 tech executive who is one of my investment partners on multiple real estate projects, falls directly in this camp. Matt's passion for this space has been evident since the first day I met him at an investment dinner for a local winery. The more I got to know him, the more amazed I was at how non-linear his life has been compared to mine. The younger Matt can be found on YouTube playing in a rock band in front of thousands, whereas the slightly older Matt worked his way into his Fortune 50 executive position, where he oversees an experience technology group. In his spare time, he is an accomplished Brazilian Jiu Jitsu competitor, a bestselling author on management execution, a TEDx presenter, a co-owner of an amazing winery, and a board member of various tech startups.

Matt's greatest strength is that he thinks a few standard deviations differently than the average person. Sometimes this can be challenging for a very linear investor like me, but most of the time, it's undeniably beneficial to our partnership. I remember when we first discussed investing in syndications passively. The next day, Matt had a working algorithm protype to evaluate what our next deal should be based on our current portfolio and our intended weightings. He reminded me of a true Ray Dalio disciple.

When I entered into my investment partnership with Matt, I never envisioned investing in anything remotely close to tech startups. It felt too much like gambling with my money. But Matt was persistent, and he educated me to the point where I no longer felt like a complete novice. Before our first start-up investment, he half-jokingly promised that everything would be okay by *assuring* me that we had a 1% chance of seeing an enormous multiple, a 4% chance of it becoming an "okay" investment, and a 95% chance of never seeing our principal again. Those odds weren't great, but with Matt's expertise and our shared solid foundation in safer assets, our risk/reward profile was probably not as dramatic as it could've been.

The more I thought about it, the high risk/high reward scenario that Matt described was exactly what my portfolio had been missing. Most of my existing real estate deals at the time had positive track records and proven models with the inverse risk/reward structure. While the approach may sound counterintuitive, adding an investment with a high-risk profile made my portfolio both more diverse and less risky at the same time.

This chapter is for the Matts out there who feel comfortable in dealing with the unknowns that have yet to be discovered. You are the visionaries. I just hope to be a part of the ride.

What Is the Asset?
A startup is when a new private company that has a limited track record but high profit potential seeks capital from investors to help scale their idea. In exchange for a capital infusion, the investor receives a share of ownership—typically a limited partnership—in the company. These investments are typically done in escalating stages, with a revalue of the company occurring after each stage.

If the company turns out be profitable, the investor is able to participate in the upside. If the company loses money or goes out of business, the losses are limited to the investor's initial investment. This is similar to how other syndications work.

What Is the History of the Asset?

The United States is a leading player in venture capital (VC) investments all around the world. This is no surprise given the country's deep history of fostering innovation through private funds.

In fact, the Industrial Revolution was ushered in by a group of New England investors known as The Boston Associates, an informal group of investors who were willing to make risky financial bets on unproven new technology[35] in developing textile companies, railroads, and banks. There's also evidence of pooling capital, partnerships, and long tail investments dating back to the whaling industry in the 18th century[36]—all of which are versions of the modern-day syndications that we've discussed in previous chapters. In particular, those long tail investments were the precursors to the strategy that Matt taught me about, which involves mixing projects marked by a high probability of failure with others that are extremely profitable in order to make up for losses and provide an above-average return over the portfolio's entire life span. It's important to note that these portfolios can remain flat for an extended period before you hit a home run on one of the investments and experience a sudden vertical spike in returns (see the following graph for an example).

---

[35] Robert F. Dalzell, *Enterprising elite: The Boston Associates and the world they made* (Cambridge, MA: Harvard University Press, 1987).

[36] Tom Nicholas and Jonas Peter Akins, "Whaling ventures," (Harvard Business School Case 813-086, October 2012).

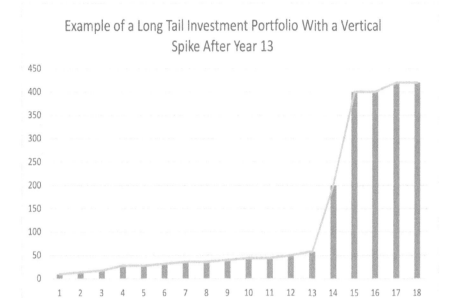

Example of a Long Tail Investment Portfolio With a Vertical
Spike After Year 13

By the 19th century, Cleveland, Ohio, had become a hotspot for innovation when prominent financiers like Andrew Mellon hand-picked entrepreneurs and financed their operations. Mellon not only invested, but he also took on active roles in the companies in his portfolio.[37] While this limited the volume of deals Mellon could do, his actions set a precedent for investors to be able to actively participate in their own deals.

In the 20th century, the idea of venture capital began to take shape, as the long tail business model proved viable. When an investor hears the term "tech startups," they automatically conjure visions of Silicon Valley when, in fact, it's the opposite coast that deserves

---

[37] Naomi R. Lamoreaux, Margaret C. Levenstein, and Kenneth L. Sokoloff, "Mobilizing venture capital during the second Industrial Revolution: Cleveland, Ohio, 1870–1920," *Capitalism and Society* 1 (2006).

much of the credit for this asset class. The modern-day VC concept gained footing on the East Coast in 1946, when members of The New England Council incorporated American Research and Development (ARD). Its illustrious members included Karl Compton, president of the Massachusetts Institute of Technology (MIT); Ralph Flanders, president of the Federal Research Bank in Boston and later senator from Vermont; Merrill Griswold, head of Massachusetts Investments Trust; and Donald K. David, dean of the Harvard Business School. Edwin R. Gilliland, head of the chemical engineering department at MIT, and Jerome C. Hunsaker, head of the aeronautical engineering department at MIT, served as technical consultants.[38] As someone who likes to consider himself an accomplished networker, I'm humbled at the thought of that scale of human capital and geographic focus.

Right after its incorporation, ARD set out to raise $5 million. While the founders attracted money from investment companies, insurance firms, educational institutions, and brokers, the majority of their funding came from individuals—which at that time was rather unique since most investment companies depended on high net-worth families for capital. Next, ARD set up systemized approaches to vetting deals with a technical advisory board that ensured that each deal was economically sound and represented the potential for significant future profit. The company also formed the proper legal structure, which included securing the necessary patents to support their products. It helped that their board of directors was diversified with some of the best legal, financial, and

---

[38] Georges F. Doriot, "American research and development papers," (Boston: Harvard Business School Baker Library Historical Collections, 1951), https://www.library.hbs.edu/hc/doriot/innovation-vc/ard/.

technological minds at MIT and Harvard. It also helped that most deals that ARD initially funded had strong ties to MIT.

ARD implemented an Andrew Mellon-inspired approach by taking an active role in its portfolio companies. And ARD's first president, Georges Doriot, signaled that he knew that what they were doing deviated from the industry's norms when he stated, "ARD does not invest in the ordinary sense. Rather, it creates by taking calculated risks in selected companies in whose growth it believes."[39] But Doriot understood that if ARD could be the backbone for these new companies, both parties would thrive. "Research and development, new technical ideas, and young small businesses are not in themselves the certain keys to great success," he said. "They must be supplemented by sound management, adequate financing, competent production methods, and aggressive merchandising."[40]

Over the next decade, ARD's initial deals provided average returns. Then came along Digital Equipment Corporation (DEC), founded by engineer/entrepreneur Harlan Anderson and MIT engineer Kenneth Olsen. DEC created circuit boards that were considerably cheaper than anything in the market, and the investment turned out to be the home run ARD was looking for. Without DEC's investment, the total portfolio from 1946–1971 produced a 7.4%

---

[39] Spencer E. Ante, *Creative capital: Georges Doriot and the birth of venture capital* (Boston: Harvard Business Press, 2008).

[40] Georges F. Doriot, "American research and development papers," (Boston: Harvard Business School Baker Library Historical Collections, 1951), https://www.library.hbs.edu/hc/doriot/innovation-vc/ard/.

annualized return; with DEC, those returns jumped to 14.7%.[41] The significance of that deal can't be overstated. By comparison, the Dow Jones Industrial Average produced a very healthy 12.8% return during that same time period.[42] The DEC investment proved that the long tail portfolio approach can beat the market if you can select the right operators and actively govern the best group until the capital event. When the venture capital industry was trying to build out its experimental new model of investing, this concept was the catalyst that spawned the market as we know it today. Many of Georges Doriot's students and ARD members went on to start their own firms, including a few that went onto San Francisco. Eventually, the Northeast region's conservative reputation worked against it, creating a window for Silicon Valley to exploit its "openness" to new ideas and become the de facto capital of the venture capital world.

What Are the Current Regulations on Buying and Selling the Asset?

There are three paths for investing in startups. One is to invest through a VC firm. Since the JOBS Act, there has been an increase in online VC firms that perform the same duties as a traditional VC firm but also offer an easy-to-use online portal. Most of these online VC funds are only open to accredited investors.

---

[41] David H. Hsu and Martin Kenney, "Organizing venture capital: The rise and demise of American Research & Development Corporation, 1946-1973," *Industrial and Corporate Change* 14, 4 (2005): 579–616.

[42] Ibid.

The second way to invest is via crowdfunding platforms. There is a section in the JOBS Act that permits non-accredited investors to invest in startups subject to certain restrictions. The investment amount can be very small compared to the majority of typical minimum investment amounts presented in this book—some as low as $100!

The third option involves a direct investment in a startup, which typically happens when you personally know the founder(s) and/or if you're a professional angel investor.

> **PRO TIP**: *A word of caution: Just because you can invest in a shiny object doesn't mean that you should. Just like any other alternative investment, you should focus on the operator rather than the platform. I have personally been burned in the past by confusing this issue. But when I invested in my startup, I personally knew the operator from the real estate world. And while the deal ultimately landed on a crowdfunding platform, my partner Matt had already vetted the deal, and we both had multiple calls with the operator prior to investing. So prior to considering any investment, make sure it's not the portal that's selling you the deal—instead, it's your background or your own personal "Matt" that helps the deal make sense to you. Otherwise, move on to the next chapter.*

What Is the Market for the Asset?

In the startup space, as in other asset classes, the ability to sell your ownership is referred to as liquidity. The first liquidity event occurs if the startup goes out of business. In this case, calculating your return is very simple: You walk away with nothing. The second liquidity event occurs if the startup is purchased privately, which usually yields great returns on your investment. The third and largest liquidity event occurs if the company is taken public on the stock market; this usually represents a considerable multiple on your returns.

Ideally, you want to hold on to your highest performers in this class. And most of the time, between the investment and the liquidity event, there really isn't a major market in which to sell your equity anyway unless the company is clearly moving toward an initial public offering (IPO), like we've seen with Airbnb and Uber during the last few years. But keep in mind that over the last decade, some of the most well-known companies—including LinkedIn, Yelp, Facebook, and Twitter—created tremendous multiples privately that were never matched publicly. Twitter, in particular, provided an 800x return privately, but has only doubled in value once since its IPO in 2013 (at the time of this publication).

In terms of liquidity in this asset class, the best defense is a good offense—which means avoiding over-allocating your portfolio to this space in the first place. And if you decide to place a small percentage of your total assets into a portfolio of startups, then you need to give that "slice of the pie" a chance to accomplish its intended purpose. For me, it's currently less than 1% of my total portfolio; while it may increase slightly from here, it will always remain proportionally small given my limited personal tech background. An important rule of thumb is the allocation should never be so high that you find yourself needing to sell a winning asset to cover a losing one.

The Bad Apples: Has Anybody Committed Fraud in This Asset Class?

Yes. Startups are valued based on different benchmarks set by the industry, and there are scores of companies that manipulate their data to convince shareholders and potential investors that their technology is extremely valuable. The manipulated data overinflates valuations, and the investors are left holding an empty bag.

What Are the Lessons to Be Learned?

At the end of the day, invest in an operator that you or the person vetting the deal can trust. The odds of hitting a home run are low, but you should be able to at least swing for the fences with an honest pitch.

The Pros and Cons of Tech Startup Investing

PROS

- Potential for outsized returns
- Great for investors that have a background in the relevant startup industry
- Can invest with a very small amount through online platforms

CONS

- Potential for 100% loss
- Can take years to materialize

ASK THE EXPERTS: Q&A With Matthew Canning

Disclaimer: This Q&A is provided for informational purposes only. You should seek your own advice from professional advisors, including lawyers, financial advisors, and accountants, regarding the legal, tax, and financial implications of any investment you contemplate.

Matthew Canning is a seasoned Fortune 50 technology executive, leadership/execution strategist, and author of several personal development books, including Foundations of Execution. *Matthew has extensive experience with residential real estate, syndications, technology startups, and private lending.*

When did you start investing?

I won't count baseball card collecting as a kid. When I was a young software engineer, I contributed a bit of money to a 401(k), although I didn't understand it at all. There was a guy who worked there that seemed like a really interesting character—he had several Porsches and rolled into the office every few days, seemingly on his own schedule. One day, I walked into his office and basically asked him what his deal was. It turned out he was a friend of the CEO's, and he happened to be an expert in a specific aspect of regulation that was critical to the company, so he was acting as a part-time consultant, as a favor. We ended up talking for a while, and I learned that he had invested in a rental property in his early twenties—before he even bought a home for himself—and had scaled until he had a completely passive and significant income stream years later.

Having come from a blue-collar "work and save" family and having focused on technology in college, I was incredibly financially ignorant, and this was the first time I really considered the power of passive income. I value freedom and the ability to pursue what I find interesting and fulfilling, and so I began to set passive income goals and experiment with different vehicles in my twenties.

My first significant investment was in a single-family property that I rehabbed, rented out for a while, and eventually sold. I hated it, and it taught me that I was much more interested in true passive vehicles than I was in semi-passive.

How were you introduced to tech startups?

By the time I had the money to invest in anything risky, I had already been a software engineer, web developer, network architect, manager, director, etc., and had developed the skill set necessary to assess technology startups. I was tuned into market needs, was able to fact check a company's adoption predictions and business plans, could poke holes in their valuations and software or network architectures, assess the abilities of the leadership team, and do everything else required to make an informed decision. For a long time, I was closely tied in with the Philadelphia tech startup community, and through that, I'd had a few opportunities to invest in a few startups over the years, but passed on many before I believed in one enough to commit money.

What is the biggest negative you discovered?

If you're only in it for the money, don't bother, because then tech startups are truly like playing the lottery—even if you choose the *right startups and they're offering the right terms, you're usually looking at a very low chance of profit.*

It's for that reason that I see startup investing as a component of a well-rounded portfolio only for those who a) are in a position to assume real risk; and b) have an area of expertise that they can pursue.

By the former, I mean this: As an example, if you can save $50 to invest, depending on your goals and life phase, a good example breakdown may be: $5 in yourself (continued education/development/tools), $15 in low risk/low return investments, $30 in medium risk/medium return, and $10 in high risk/high return. Startups fall squarely into the last category. But if you're not able to save enough to meet your primary investing objectives, high risk/high return may very well be the first to go.

For the latter, I happen to understand technology well enough to give me an advantage over randomness when vetting technology startups, so that's my niche. You may be in a position where your expertise in (or interest in) anything from real estate to sports to music will give you a similar advantage, and by limiting the scope of the investments you consider to those that fall within your sweet spot, you're using information to minimize risk as best you can within an inherently risky asset type. You can always pull in others for advice relating to the operations or technologies that facilitate transactions, but—when it comes to individual investments as opposed to managed funds—you should natively understand the primary domain in which the startup operates.

What is your most memorable experience in this asset class?

In many cases, when I invest in a startup, I also get involved in a limited capacity as an advisor—even if that simply means that I'm available should they need me. I always find it fulfilling when I give a startup's leaders advice, they heed it, and we collectively see the positive results of that advice come to fruition. Without citing any particular example, that's consistently been my most positive experience in this space.

What is a common misconception about tech startups?

That you have to be an experienced technologist to get your feet wet. See my above comment—you should be experienced in whatever domain the startup operates in, but innovation and disruption can occur in any industry.

What is the most important thing an investor should know when considering a tech startup?

Pay attention to your gut when it comes to assessing whether or not the leadership team has what it takes. Experience is great, but agility, the ability to learn, to seek out and accept critical feedback, etc., are absolutely critical, regardless of age and experience.

What is your professional background, and how did it affect your investing career?

My background in software engineering provided a perspective: a systems approach to complexity. Whether assessing a publicly traded security, a real estate deal, or a startup, it's been valuable to be able to apply the same principles and perceive things as systems of systems—risks, personalities, financial considerations, technologies, locations, external and market factors, etc.—as well as its place in a multi-dimensional landscape that includes its current place in time, its history, likely future paths, etc.

What information sources have been the most influential for you?

Some podcasts that aren't necessarily business-focused, but which consistently broaden my perspective, are Sam Harris' Making Sense due to the quality of the guests and the fact that it goes deep into longform conversations. I got hooked when I heard episode #34, which featured a philosopher I follow named David Chalmers, and then listened consistently until COVID stopped me from commuting and, therefore, enjoying dedicated podcast time. I also enjoy the Artificial Intelligence podcast with Lex Fridman for the same reason. I also need to call out Story Pirates as influential, because when I put it on in the car, my kids focus on it, and that affords me a few minutes to collect my thoughts without being forced into conversations about Harry Potter or Minecraft.

One book that I'd recommend to anyone involved with business or investing is Principles by Ray Dalio. And if you're too lazy or busy to read it, it's also available in a shorter form as a series of animated YouTube videos.

For investing in startups in particular, spend some time learning about incubators, SAFEs, convertible notes, etc. Just find some video walkthroughs and start from there. Even if you don't end up exploring the asset type, it's good to know how such contractual vehicles work because they'll give you a broader perspective about other types of equity contracts, PPMs, etc.

Who that you personally know do you most respect in business, and why?

I used to work for a man who, in his youth, wrote down five ideas on a yellow sticky note that he kept in his wallet. No one saw the note. He was spending his life working his way down it from top to bottom. The first one was a business that he sold for millions. I worked for him at the second. I don't know how he's doing, but I've always admired that singularity of focus.

You are at a holiday party and asked what you do for a living. What do you say?

I'd respond by saying, "eh, a few different things," and see where the conversation goes from there. Investing is a means to the life that I choose to live. Technology is an interest and something that I've developed enough of an acumen with that I can provide value. I'm most fulfilled when I'm exercising creativity or helping others— whether developing leaders or individuals—work toward their goals. And so my answer isn't cut and dried, and that is something I'm grateful for.

What is the best piece of investing advice that you've ever received?

The best advice I ever heard is incredibly simple and comes by way of a cliché: "The best time to invest in real estate is yesterday." While that advice speaks to the fact that time affects real estate *positively (via appreciation), it applies to nearly any investment. The sooner you invest in a real estate syndication, the sooner you'll have your principal returned and can reinvest while reaping the benefits of your LP ownership stake. And this applies to startups, as well, because of the time it takes between investing and a company being able to turn a profit (if they do at all).*

What's your greatest alternative investment failure, and what would you do differently?

While the amount lost wasn't heart-stopping, as far as sheer percentage of portfolio loss, my greatest alternative investment failure has been in the niche cryptocurrency space. I had done my homework and believed that I was buying at a sound point. It turned out the market had a lot of room to drop. I'm hanging on, though!

In five years, do you still see yourself investing in this niche?

Yes, absolutely. It's a great intersection of my interests and knowledge, and it fits cleanly into my current risk-diversification strategy.

ASK THE EXPERTS: Q&A With Jeremy Davis

Disclaimer: This Q&A is provided for informational purposes only. You should seek your own advice from professional advisors, including lawyers, financial advisors, and accountants, regarding the legal, tax, and financial implications of any investment you contemplate.

Jeremy Davis has been a technology professional for 20+ years. He feels fortunate that his passion for investing was timed perfectly with the rapidly accelerating technology industry. Jeremy makes investments under his own due diligence, by way of trends that he follows or introductions from his connections.

When did you start investing?

Lightly in 2009, and then much deeper starting in 2015.

How were you introduced to tech startups?

I was gifted a book on computer programming at age 9 and never looked back. Software development has been my profession since the late '90s, so it was a natural area for me to invest in.

What is the biggest negative you discovered?

There's a tendency in technology firms to spend a lot of money before finding a way to stabilize profitability. This just means you need to choose your company and founder(s) wisely.

What is your most memorable experience in this asset class?

Being involved with a company when it's ten people or less in a small office and then returning three to five years later to see 150+ employees occupying an entire building or floor of a building. It's remarkable to be a part of that and witness the momentum behind something that starts so small.

What is the most important thing an investor should know when considering a tech startup?

Invest in the founder/team more than the product. A good founder will pivot as necessary, and a strong team will ensure a quality result.

What information sources have been the most influential for you?

Personal networks, hands down. The more people you know, the more you meet. Personal introductions are always the most valuable, especially when they come from people who you respect, and vice versa.

Who that you personally know do you most respect in business, and why?

Mike Speiser of Sutter Hill Ventures. A true class act of a businessman and human being. We worked closely together for several years, and he has since gone on to launch several tremendously successful businesses.

You are at a holiday party and asked what you do for a living. What do you say?

I'm a semi-retired software developer and investor.

What is the best piece of investing advice that you've ever received?

Prioritizing investing in the founder/team above the product has proven prescient time and time again.

What's your greatest alternative investment failure, and what would you do differently?

I got involved investing in a space that I didn't have much experience in. Instead of doing a significant amount of my own due diligence, I took the word of the officers at the company as well as that of a third party. Furthermore, I invested quite a bit more money than I should have, given my relative inexperience. In the future, keeping investment allocations like these small and putting in the requisite amount of research is a must.

In five years, do you still see yourself investing in this niche?

Yes, hopefully!

TAKEAWAYS

- Investing in startups with private financing has a long history in the United States
- A long tail investment strategy is an advanced approach that looks for well calculated home runs
- Make sure you have a good understanding of the business and the operators
- Both accredited and non-accredited investors can invest in this space

12

TO BE OR NOT TO BE ACCREDITED?

Put simply, becoming an accredited investor should be a goal for all investors because it provides them with access to a much better selection of deals. In addition, accredited investors typically have a strong enough financial footing that they can absorb a few bad investments without suffering a personal financial hardship. You'll find that learning from bad investments is a critical step in becoming a better investor. Contrary to what a financial advisor may tell you, everyone makes mistakes—*especially* financial professionals. But those mistakes will directly lead to improving your knowledge of investing, and that will have positive ripple effects for the rest of your life.

For these reasons, most of the alternative investments mentioned in this book are geared toward accredited investors. However, if you don't yet meet the criteria for accreditation, here is a summary of the assets we covered that are still available to you:

- High-equity life insurance policies
- Individual long-term mortgage notes [not funds]
- Mobile home parks [506(b) or joint venture]
- Self-storage [506(b) or joint venture]

- Apartment buildings [506(b) or joint venture]
- Startups [via Title III of the JOBS Act; restrictions apply]
- Individual ATM machines [not funds]

Note: If you are a non-accredited investor strictly looking to remain passive, you should avoid getting into deals that would require a large time commitment, such as a joint venture. In all cases, you'll want to follow the same basic guidelines as you would on any investment: learn as much as you can about every opportunity, conduct due diligence, network, and don't rush into anything that seems too good to be true.

If I decide to write a follow-up book, it will certainly feature additions to this list and updates on the assets mentioned here. Just like you, I am always expanding my investment knowledge, both through my experiences and through my network.

13

BEST PRACTICES FOR NETWORKING

If I have emphasized one strategy for success above all others throughout this book, it is networking. You simply cannot achieve sustainable positive results in the alternative investing space without mastering this skill. Here is how I personally approach networking, and I believe this model can work for anyone.

- Use LinkedIn to learn the language of your niche: Simply add the words "alternative investor" or "real estate investor" to your profile. After a few weeks, you'll routinely receive requests to schedule calls with your growing LinkedIn network. In all honesty, I received very little true value from these calls, but I did get the vital practice that I needed in discussing investment topics. You'll want to scale back the LinkedIn calls as your actual organic network grows.

- Go to conferences that feature a large list of operators speaking. While there, don't worry about networking with a large quantity of attendees. Instead, strive for fewer high-quality conversations. It helps to find a commonality to discuss, such as, "Hey, we invested in the same operator. How has your experience been?" Caveat: Be very honest about your investment background, even if you have never invested in a single deal. Ask for your new contact's business card and jot down a few things you discussed. After the conference, take out all of the business cards and email every single person using the notes you made. My first conference was a three-day event that included at least 16 hours of networking. Afterward, I emailed about 25–30 people in the hotel room before checking out. Out of that group, I built subsequent relationships with six contacts.

-   Once you have four to six people in your organic network, ask to schedule a call with them every couple of months, and **put it on your calendar**. Send them a calendar invite, as well. Never say to a contact, "Stay in touch." It's so lazy, and it will never get you anywhere. Instead, get in the habit of saying something specific like, "How about a call in three months to see how things worked out with XYZ deal?" Usually, once a quarter is a great benchmark for these types of calls, but use your judgment. They can be more frequent with contacts with whom you have a good rapport, and less frequent with those with whom you don't click as well. Also, move people you have made no personal connection with to an email follow-up list. If you notice a few well-spaced emails getting no responses, by all means, just delete the person from your network.

You might be wondering if this is different from the LinkedIn calls mentioned above, and the answer is a resounding *yes*. This is because you have already exchanged emails, and both you and the investor have started to invest in a relationship. A great habit to get into is jotting down notes after every call as a starting point for the next conversation. You might not think you have too much to offer at this point, but if you listen to what the other investor is doing, there's usually an opportunity to help somehow. For example, Investor A tells you he's looking to invest in real estate in the Charlotte, NC, market to diversify his locations. Coincidentally, one of the other five investors you have been exchanging emails with has just mentioned that he just invested in a deal in the same city. Your job is to make the introduction and expect nothing in return. This is the trick to networking! The returns from the relationships you build will come back around 100-fold, and you'll be amazed at how quickly your network begins to grow.

- Listen to one alternative investment podcast every day. A few of the experts featured in this book have excellent options to consider. When you hear something that genuinely resonates with you, reach out and tell the hosts or guests about it. It is common for them to provide their contact information, and they do so for this very reason. Their goal is to connect with others in their investment space, and they will welcome the chance to get to know you. Just remember: Their job is not to be your coach or to teach you everything they know; rather, it's just to see where the relationship goes organically.

14
CLOSING THOUGHTS

This year, I will turn 34. It will mark the 20th anniversary of my first investment. It's true that time goes fast, but experiences and knowledge are learned slow. In 2021, I leveraged those 20 years of experience into creating my private equity fund, SIH Capital Group. My mission was to provide accredited investors with a simple, transparent income source that is supported not simply by one individual asset class, but rather by five distinct asset classes that complement each other's pros and cons. The result is a well-diversified income machine that primarily focuses on the real estate investments mentioned in this book.

Similarly, one of my primary motives for writing this book was to be able to share with investors that a world of opportunities exists right under their noses—I like to think of it as a "Narnia" for investors. The best part is that the pros and cons associated with alternative investments overlap each other in so many ways that learning one alternative asset class mentioned in this book substantially decreases the learning curve for the next investment. If you factor in that you can leverage your professional background when approaching some of these assets (a software engineer who invests in a tech startup), that learning curve gets flattened exponentially.

To be fair and balanced, I wanted to make sure that the cons of the investments received just as much attention as the pros. In every chapter, I also provided examples of fraud and misconceptions about each asset class. While alternative investments, as a whole, are often unfairly likened to Ponzi schemes, that's simply not the case. Keep in mind that it's not the asset class that commits the fraud; it's the operators that do. And bad apples in this space don't take away from all of the excellent operators out there who are putting their investors first.

Thank you for following this conversation through to the end. I hope you got as much out of reading this book as I got out of writing it. Be well and happy investing.

GLOSSARY

1031 exchange — The process of deferring tax liability by rolling over gains from one real estate project to another. Usually facilitated by a third-party intermediary.

Accredited investor — An investor that meets the criteria set by the U.S. Securities and Exchange Commission and financial regulation laws in order to qualify for making certain investments.

Alternative asset/investment — An asset/investment that is not categorized as a traditional investment and would not be found in a standard investment portfolio. Examples are real estate, art, jewelry, and private equity funds.

Angel investor — A high net-worth individual who provides funding for start-up companies, often in exchange for an equity share in them. Also called a private or seed investor.

Arbitrage — To make a profit by simultaneously buying and selling the same asset in two different markets.

Bitcoins — A digital currency that serves as a ledger for recorded transactions.

Blue-chip stock — The stock of a company that is deemed to be of the highest quality with a long-standing favorable track record.

Capital event — A large return of investment capital to an investor. For life insurance policy settlements, this usually occurs when the beneficiary passes; for commercial real estate, it happens at the time of sale or refinance of a property.

Capitalization rate — A multiple of what the market is willing to pay for the profitability of a business/property.

Cash flow — The cash earned by an investment. This is usually measured by subtracting all expenses from all revenue. This number can be negative if expenses are higher than revenue.

Cash value — The cash available to an insurance policyholder for surrender or loan purposes.

Champerty — A doctrine that prevents a person with no involvement in a lawsuit from offering to assist in its prosecution or defense in exchange for a share of the proceeds of the suit. The law is intended to discourage frivolous lawsuits.

Closed-end funds (CEFs) — A fund model that sells a fixed number of shares and then goes on to execute its business model which usually involves debt instruments. CEFs are allowed to use leverage in order to increase the yield of the fund.

Collateralization — The process of leveraging one asset to purchase another asset without having to sell the original asset.

Commodity — An economic item that can be used to exchange for other economic items. Most common examples are gold, oil, and currencies.

Cost segregation — Breaking down the depreciation into individual components allowing for a higher depreciation amount in a project's early years.

Crowdfunding — The pooling of modest sums of capital from a large number of individuals that are used to finance a new business startup or other project.

Depreciation — The reduction of the value of the asset due to wear and tear.

Due diligence — The process prior to investing of evaluating the key variables needed for an investment to be successful.

Duplex — Two rental units in one building.

Financial Independence, Retire Early (FIRE) — A movement popularized by millennials that retired from their jobs at an untraditionally early age.

First lien position — Senior debt on a property that takes priority in repayment over other liens on the property.

Four D's of Life — Death, divorce, downsizing, and dislocation. These variables produce a positive business environment for some investments, such as the self-storage industry.

General partner — The operator of a deal that sources, manages, and executes on a business plan and usually has 100% control of operations.

High-equity cash value policy — Otherwise known as the Infinite Banking Concept (IBC), is a whole life insurance policy from a mutual life insurance company designed to maximize the cash value of the policy instead of the death benefit.

Independent ATM Deployer (IAD) — A centralization of ATM machines that are not associated with major banks.

Initial Public Offering (IPO) — The process of a private company offering new ownership shares to be sold on public stock exchanges.

Insurable interest — Refers to proof that an insurance policy owner would suffer financial hardship if the insured suffered an adverse event. Most commonly, you see this interest easily established by spouses, children, parents, and business partners.

Internal rate of return (IRR) — A method of calculating an investment's average rate of return factoring in the time value of money and the investments cash flow schedule.

Joint venture — A joint venture deal requires an investor to have an active role in the project. It is a great way to transition from being a passive investor to an active investor.

Junior (second position) lien — Also known as a second mortgage, this is borrowing that occurs after a first lien is already in place. The debt is ranked by order in the event of a borrower's bankruptcy and liquidation. Second lien debt repayment is made after first lien debt is fully repaid.

Leverage — The proportion of debt to equity. Leverage is a double-edged sword: Too little lowers an investor's overall returns, while too much puts them at risk of default if the market goes down.

Life settlement — The process of a life insurance policy owner selling their policy to an investor in exchange for a lump sum payment that is generally less than the policy's death benefit, but more than its cash surrender value. This payment usually takes into account the insured's age, health, life expectancy, and the terms and conditions of the policy.

Limited partner — An investor in a deal that is usually passive in nature and has no operational authority.

Liquidity — The ability to sell an asset at any given time. Stocks are considered very liquid, while private equity investments are considered relatively illiquid because they take longer to sell.

Long tail investment portfolio — A strategy of investing in projects that have a high probability of failure; the projects that succeed are extremely profitable in order to make up for any losses and provide an above-average return for an entire portfolio.

Master limited partnership — A hybrid corporate structure that incorporates the tax benefits of a private partnership with the liquidity of a company traded on the stock market.

Mastermind — A group of like-minded individuals getting together to share their experiences and ideas with each other.

Modified endowment contract (MEC) — The modified tax structure and IRS classification of a life insurance policy whose cumulative premiums exceed federal tax law limits (see **Seven-pay test**).

Net operating income (NOI) — A formula used to show how profitable a business is by subtracting all the revenue the business produces from all reasonably necessary operating expenses.

Non-performing note — A note that is more than 90 days past due.

Non-recourse mortgage — A real estate loan for which the investor is not liable if the borrower defaults, unless there is evidence of fraud or similar activity.

Note — A contractual agreement to repay a loan between a borrower and a lender based on set terms.

Note-servicing company — A company that takes care of the monthly management of note payments.

Options — A contract to buy or sell a stock at a later time, allowing an investor to leverage their bets.

Owner financing — When a seller agrees to hold an entire mortgage note or a portion thereof.

Park-owned mobile homes — Comparable to a traditional apartment. The owner of the home is responsible for all repairs and maintenance, in exchange for the tenant paying higher rental fees. The home belongs to the park.

Partial note — The investor can sell a portion of the income that is coming from the note. This can be done as a percentage of the existing yield or a fixed stream of income for a set number of years.

Performing note — A note that is current in all payment obligations or less than 90 days past due.

Preferred return — A preferred return is the hurdle that an investor needs to see in distributions before the investor starts splitting the profits with the operator.

Pro forma — A Latin term meaning "for the sake of form," this is a method of calculating financial results, based on specific projections or presumptions, that is used by managers or investors to make decisions.

Property management — The person/company responsible for the oversight of a property. Property management can be handled by an operator or an outside vendor.

Real estate investment trust (REIT) — A publicly traded company that purchases and manages real estate-focused businesses. Apartment REITS are usually end buyers from larger private syndicators who tend to purchase large complexes that have been stabilized and are receiving close to the maximum market rent prior to their acquisition.

Reperforming note — A note that was previously delinquent but is now paid up to date.

Rule 506(b) of Regulation D — An exemption that states that an operator may not openly advertise their deals, but they may sell their securities to an unlimited number of accredited investors and up to 35 non-accredited "sophisticated investors" that have a level of knowledge and experience that qualifies them to make informed decisions about entering into such agreements.

Rule 506(c) of Regulation D — An exemption that states that an operator is free to advertise their deals in a 506(c) offering as long as all investors are accredited, and the operator has taken reasonable steps to verify their accredited status.

Seven-pay test — A formula for determining whether the total amount of premiums paid into a life insurance policy at any point in the first seven years of the contract exceeds what would be required to have the policy paid up in seven years. This test is used to classify a policy as an MEC (see **Modified endowment contract)** and to prevent life insurance policies from being used as tax shelters.

Sophisticated investor — Someone who has the experience, net worth, and necessary capital to be able to effectively evaluate the risk/reward profiles of more advanced deals.

Syndication — The pooling together of money to purchase a common asset. A common syndication will have a limited partner and a general partner.

Tenant-owned mobile homes — Comparable to a traditional homeowner. The tenant just rents the lot and is responsible for all repairs and maintenance, but the home belongs to the tenant.

Term life insurance — A life insurance policy that provides coverage to an individual for a specifically designated time period in exchange for a fixed rate of payments.

Time value of money — A principle that states that the money you currently have on hand is worth more than the same sum in the future due to its immediate earning potential.

Value-add deal — A deal that requires corrective action to fully maximize its business potential.

Value stock — A stock trading at a low multiple compared to its earnings. The designation tends to lend itself to older companies that pay higher dividends because their businesses have matured.

Viatical settlement — A life insurance settlement involving the chronic or terminally ill.

Volatility — The speed and degree of fluctuation in the price of an asset.

Whole life insurance — A permanent life insurance policy that is designed to provide coverage for the entire life of the insured.

REFERENCES

Self-Storage Almanac. Phoenix, AZ: MiniCo, 2020-2021.

"Accredited Investors - Updated Investor Bulletin," Investor.gov (April 14, 2021), https://www.investor.gov/introduction-investing/general-resources/news-alerts/alerts-bulletins/investor-bulletins/updated-3.

Amadeo, Kimberly. "Mortgage history, types, and impact on the economy," The Balance (February 26, 2021), https://www.thebalance.com/what-is-a-mortgage-types-history-impact-3305946.

"An overview of self-storage law," Inside Self-Storage, March 1, 2005, https://www.insideselfstorage.com/archive/overview-self-storage-law.

Ante, Spencer E. *Creative capital: Georges Doriot and the birth of venture capital* (Boston: Harvard Business Press, 2008).

Bátiz-Lazo, Bernardo. "A brief history of the ATM," *The Atlantic* (March 26, 2015), https://www.theatlantic.com/technology/archive/2015/03/a-brief-history-of-the-atm/388547/.

Bellis, Mary. "The history of mobile homes," ThoughtCo (March 5, 2019), https://www.thoughtco.com/history-of-mobile-homes-4076982.

Bennett, Sydney. "Are manufactured homes a solution to the housing affordability crisis?", Apartment List (June 15, 2018), https://www.apartmentlist.com/research/mobile-homes-affordability-crisis.

Bradley, Alice. "A brief history of the apartment," REA Group (July 12, 2016), https://www.realestate.com.au/news/brief-history-apartment-living/.

Buffett, Warren E. *Berkshire Hathaway annual report* (February 28, 2005), https://www.berkshirehathaway.com/letters/2004ltr.pdf.

Caucci, Raymond. "Penn Mutual continues historic dividend track record." *Penn Mutual Perspectives* (December 15, 2020), https://blog.pennmutual.com/penn-mutual-continues-historic-dividend-track-record/.

Cooley, Philip L., Hubbard, Carl M., and Walz, Daniel T. "Retirement savings: Choosing a withdrawal rate that is sustainable," American Association of Individual Investors (1998), https://www.aaii.com/files/pdf/6794_retirement-savings-choosing-a-withdrawal-rate-that-is-sustainable.pdf.

Dalzell, Robert F. *Enterprising elite: The Boston Associates and the world they made* (Cambridge, MA: Harvard University Press, 1987).

Doriot, Georges F. "American research and development papers," (Boston: Harvard Business School Baker Library Historical Collections, 1951), https://www.library.hbs.edu/hc/doriot/innovation-vc/ard/.

"GRIGSBY v. RUSSELL," FindLaw, https://caselaw.findlaw.com/us-supreme-court/222/149.html.

"How America banks: Household use of banking and financial services," FDIC Survey (2019), https://www.fdic.gov/analysis/household-survey/.

Hsu, David H., and Kenney, Martin. "Organizing venture capital: The rise and demise of American Research & Development Corporation, 1946-1973," *Industrial and Corporate Change* 14, 4 (2005): 579–616.

"Investor bulletin on life settlements," U.S. Securities and Exchange Commission (January 1, 2011), https://www.sec.gov/investor/alerts/lifesettlements-bulletin.htm.

Kagan, Julia. "Automated teller machine (ATM)," Investopedia (January 28, 2021), https://www.investopedia.com/terms/a/atm.asp.

Kern, Andrew. "Why manufactured housing is the new affordable housing," *Commercial Property Executive* (October 2020), https://www.cpexecutive.com/post/why-manufactured-housing-is-the-new-affordable-housing/.

Lamoreaux, Naomi R., Levenstein, Margaret C., and Sokoloff, Kenneth L. "Mobilizing venture capital during the second Industrial Revolution: Cleveland, Ohio, 1870–1920," *Capitalism and Society* 1 (2006).

"Life settlement investments: Pros and cons and facts," Partners 4 Prosperity LLC (May 19, 2017), http://partners4prosperity.com/life-settlement-investments-pros-and-cons-facts-faqs/

Lloyd, Alcynna. "Decade in review: Number of U.S. renters surpasses 100 million," HousingWire (March 12, 2020), https://www.housingwire.com/articles/decade-in-review-number-of-u-s-renters-surpasses-100-million/.

"MassMutual approves estimated 2021 policyowner dividend payout of more than $1.7 billion." MassMutual (November 2, 2020), https://www.massmutual.com/about-us/news-and-press-releases/press-releases/2020/11/MassMutual-approves-estimated-2021-policyowner-dividend-payout-of-more-than-17-billion.

Nicholas, Tom, and Akins, Jonas Peter. "Whaling ventures," (Harvard Business School Case 813-086, October 2012).

"Partial purchase note offer," Amerinote Xchange (November 17, 2020), https://www.amerinotexchange.com/partial-purchase-note-offer/.

"Seniors beware: What you should know about life settlements," FINRA (July 30, 2009), https://www.finra.org/investors/alerts/seniors-beware-what-you-should-know-about-life-settlements.

Vanderbilt, Tom. "Self-storage nation," *Slate Magazine* (July 18, 2005), https://slate.com/culture/2005/07/self-storage-in-america.html.

ABOUT THE AUTHOR

After graduating with a BBA and MBA from Baruch College in New York City, Denis Shapiro began working for the U.S. Government in a career that he proudly built for over a decade. In his various roles with the government, Denis served as a liaison to the public and various state agencies and gained a unique view of the importance of portfolio allocation and management.

Denis began investing in real estate in 2012, when the market was just beginning to recover from the global financial crisis. He went on to build a cash flowing portfolio that includes many alternative assets, such as note and ATM funds, mobile home parks, life insurance policies, tech start-ups, industrial property, short-term rentals, and more. He also co-founded an investment club for accredited investors in 2019. Leveraging these successes and the lessons learned throughout his career, Denis launched SIH Capital Group, an alternative investment fund that provides accredited investors with a simplified strategy to invest for passive income.

The Alternative Investment Almanac: Expert Insights on Building Personal Wealth in Non-Traditional Ways is based on his personal experiences, supplemented by interviews with some of the best alternative asset investors in the business today.

30133164R00173